THE
Difference
MAKER

MAKING YOUR ATTITUDE
YOUR GREATEST ASSET

JOHN C. MAXWELL

THOMAS NELSON
Since 1798

NASHVILLE   DALLAS   MEXICO CITY   RIO DE JANEIRO   BEIJING

Published in Nashville, Tennessee, by Thomas Nelson, Inc.

Nelson Books titles may be purchased in bulk for educational, business, fundraising, or sales promotional use. For information, please e-mail SpecialMarkets@ThomasNelson.com.

Scripture quotations are from THE NEW KING JAMES VERSION. Copyright © 1979, 1980, 1982, Thomas Nelson, Inc., Publishers.

Published in association with Yates & Yates, LLP, Attorneys and Counselors, Orange, California.

Library of Congress Cataloging-in-Publication Data

Maxwell, John C., 1947-
    The difference maker : making your attitude your greatest asset / John C. Maxwell.
      p. cm.
    Includes bibliographical references.
    ISBN 0-7852-6098-6 (hardcover)
    ISBN-10 0-7852-8869-4 (I.E.)
    ISBN-13 978-0-7852-8869-5 (I.E.)
    1. Attitude (Psychology) 2. Success. I. Title.
BF327.M39 2006
650.1—dc22
2006006618

Printed in the United States of America

07 08 09 RRD 10 9 8

ACKNOWLEDGMENTS

This book is dedicated to my assistants:
Barbara Brumagin (1981–1992)
&
Linda Eggers (1995–present)

Thanks for your
servant-hearts, people skills,
competence, loyalty, and friendship.
Both of you have been
Difference Makers in my life!

Thank you to
Charlie Wetzel, my writer;
Stephanie Wetzel, who proofs and
edits the manuscript; and
Linda Eggers, my assistant

CONTENTS

ONE

Where Did You Get Your Attitude?

Have you ever heard someone say, "Attitude is everything"? It seems to be a favorite line of some motivational speakers. According to them, a great attitude is all you need to be successful. Unfortunately, it's simply not true.

I do a lot of professional speaking. Each year I communicate at live events to 250,000 people. And I do believe in motivating others. However, I don't think of myself as a motivational speaker. I call myself a motivational *teacher*. That may seem like a technicality, but here's the difference: A motivational speaker makes you feel good, but the next day you're not sure why. A motivational *teacher* also makes you feel good, but the next day you possess something that will actually help you.

The promise that attitude is everything is hollow. In fact, if you believe that attitude is everything, it may actually hurt you more than help you. If attitude were everything, then the only thing that would separate me from a successful singing career would be the belief that I can do it. But trust me, there is another factor that stands in my way: talent. If you've watched the reality show *American Idol*, then you know what I mean. I am amazed at the number of terrible auditioners who respond to blunt criticism from the judges by saying things like, "I know I can sing. That's just your opinion." Truthfully, no attitude is strong enough to compensate for lack of skill.

So does a good attitude make any difference? Absolutely. Attitude is the difference maker! *Attitude isn't everything, but it is one thing that can make a difference in your life.* Businessman, philanthropist, and author W. Clement Stone stated, "There is little difference in people, but the little difference makes a big difference. The little difference is attitude. The big difference is whether it is positive or negative."

The goal of this book is not to *snow* you by saying that attitude is everything, but to *show* you that your attitude is the difference maker in your life. I desire to do that by helping you understand where your attitude comes from, what it *can* and *can't* do for you, and how you can make it an asset. I also want to give you insight into how to deal with the Big Five Attitude Obstacles everybody faces: discouragement, change, problems, fear, and failure. If you're like most people, you have to deal with at least one of those issues *every single day*! Let's take this journey together by first looking at some basics about attitude.

WHAT IS ATTITUDE?

What is an attitude, anyway? When you hear the word, what do you think about? I think of attitude as an inward feeling expressed by outward behavior. People always project on the outside what they feel on the inside. Some people try to mask their attitude, and they can fool others for a while. But that cover-up doesn't last long. Attitude always wiggles its way out.

My father loves to tell the story of a four-year-old boy who was finally put into time-out after battling his mother.

"Sit in that chair until the timer goes off," the mother said in frustration. The boy sat down, fearing greater punishment, but said, "Okay, Mommy. I'm sitting on the outside, but I'm standing up on the inside."

Your attitude colors every aspect of your life. It is like the mind's paintbrush. It can paint everything in bright, vibrant colors—creating a masterpiece. Or it can make everything dark and dreary. Attitude is so pervasive and important that I've come to think of it like this:

It is the vanguard of your true self.

Its root is inward but its fruit is outward.

It is your best friend or worst enemy.

It is more honest and consistent about you than your words.

It is your outward look based on your past experiences.

It is what draws people to you or repels them.

It is never content until it is expressed.

It is the librarian of your past.

It is the speaker of your present.

It is the prophet of your future.

There is not a single part of your current life that is not affected by your attitude. And your future will definitely be influenced by the attitude you carry with you from today forward.

> *Your attitude colors every aspect of your life.*
> *It is like the mind's paintbrush.*

WHERE DID I GET MY ATTITUDE?

If your attitude is so important, then you may be asking yourself, *Where did I get it? Am I stuck with it my whole life—for better or worse?* First, let's look at the question of where your attitude comes from.

1. PERSONALITY—WHO YOU ARE

Two men were out fishing. When the fish stopped biting, they started to talk. One man praised his wife and extolled her many virtues, summing it up by saying, "You know, if all men were like me, they would all want to be married to my wife."

"And if they were like me," the other replied, "none of them would want to be!"

Everybody's different. Each person is born a unique

individual. We're all as different as our fingerprints. That's true even of siblings born of the same parents and brought up in the same household. Even twins who are genetically identical have distinct personalities.

Your personality type—your natural "wiring"— impacts your attitude. That's not to say that you're trapped by your personality, because you're not. But your attitude is certainly impacted by it.

2. ENVIRONMENT—WHAT'S AROUND YOU

The environment you were exposed to growing up definitely has an impact on your attitude. Did your parents go through a divorce? That may cause you to have a mistrustful attitude toward members of the opposite sex. Did someone close to you die? That may prompt you to have an attitude of emotional distancing from others. Did you grow up in a poor neighborhood? That may prompt you to have a tenacious attitude toward achievement. In contrast, it could make you want to give up more easily.

It may be hard to predict exactly *what* will happen to a person's attitude based on his or her early environment, but you can be certain that it made an impact of some kind. My wife and I adopted both of our children, and based on that experience, we believe that genetics is the strongest early predictor of attitude. But we also know for a fact that environment makes a difference.

3. THE EXPRESSION OF OTHERS—WHAT YOU FEEL

Most people can remember the harsh words of a parent or teacher even years or decades after the fact. Some people carry the scars of such experiences their entire lives. In my book *Winning with People*, the Pain Principle states, "Hurting people hurt people and are easily hurt by them." Many times the hurts that cause people to overreact to others come as the result of negative words from others.

Likewise, positive words can have an impact on a person's attitude. Can you remember the positive words of a favorite teacher or other significant adult? A few words can change the way a person thinks of himself and can change the course of his life. Charlie Wetzel, my writer, remembers the words of his sister, Barbara Rensink, when he was eighteen. He had little direction in his life back then, and she told him that she thought he had a talent for cooking and how flavors go together. He had never considered that before. It sent him on a ten-year quest learning everything he could about food, cooking, and the restaurant business. And it led to his first career as a professional restaurant chef.

4. SELF-IMAGE—HOW YOU SEE YOURSELF

How you see yourself has a tremendous impact on your attitude. Poor self-image and poor attitudes often walk hand in hand. It's hard to see anything in the world as positive if you see yourself as negative.

Dwayne Dyer advises, "Examine the labels you apply to yourself. Every label is a boundary or limit you will not let yourself cross." If you are having trouble getting where you want to go, the problem may be inside you. If you don't change your inward feelings about yourself, you will be unable to change your outward actions toward others.

5. EXPOSURE TO GROWTH OPPORTUNITIES—WHAT YOU EXPERIENCE

Enlightenment writer and philosopher Voltaire likened life to a game of cards. Players must accept the cards dealt to them. However, once they have those cards in hand, they alone choose how they will play them. They decide what risks and actions to take.

The growth opportunities people experience are not all equal. When I was growing up, my parents constantly exposed me to new experiences that would shape me. They sent me to Dale Carnegie's "How to Win Friends and Influence People" and other courses while I was in junior high and high school. My father occasionally took me out of school for a week so that I could travel with him as he performed his duties as a leader of our religious denomination. He took me to hear great evangelists and missionaries speak. My parents even paid me to read books that would shape my thinking. They did everything they could to cultivate an attitude open to personal growth. As an adult I have continued to embrace that attitude and to try to pass it along to my children and grandchildren.

Not everyone is as fortunate as I was. If you had an upbringing similar to mine, thank your parents. However, if you were rarely exposed to growth experiences or taken outside of your comfort zone, then you may have to work harder to cultivate a positive attitude toward positive personal growth.

6. Association with Peers—Who You Are With

All the time you hear about young people in trouble who are said to have been nice kids who ended up hanging with the wrong crowd. It's a fact that you start becoming like the people you spend a lot of time with. If a nice kid spends all of his time with people of low moral character, it's only a matter of time before he begins to display low moral character. Likewise, if someone with a good attitude spends all her time with individuals who display negative attitudes, guess what will happen to her? She'll begin to develop a negative attitude. She may think she can change them, but if she's outnumbered and gets no relief from their negativity, they are the ones who will be doing the influencing, not her.

7. BELIEFS—WHAT YOU THINK

Many of the factors I've mentioned that have come together to shape your attitude were set in motion in your past. But do you know what forms and sustains your attitude most today? Your thoughts. As author and successful businessman Bob Conklin indicated in the following piece, thoughts make a huge impact on you:

> I can make you rise or fall. I can work for you or against you. I can make you a success or a failure.
>
> I control the way that you feel and the way that you act.
>
> I can make you laugh . . . work . . . love. I can make your heart sing with joy . . . excitement . . . elation.

Or I can make you wretched . . . dejected . . . morbid.

I can make you sick . . . listless.

I can be as a shackle . . . heavy . . . attached . . . burdensome.

Or I can be as the prism's hue . . . dancing . . . bright . . . fleeting . . . lost forever unless captured by pen or purpose.

I can be nurtured and grown to be great and beautiful . . . seen by the eyes of others through action in you.

I can never be removed . . . only replaced.

I am a THOUGHT.

Why not know me better?[1]

Every thought you have shapes your life. What you think about your neighbor is your attitude toward him. The way you think about your job is your attitude toward work. Your thoughts concerning your spouse, the people on the highway during rush hour, and the government create your attitude toward each of those subjects.

> *The sum of all your thoughts*
> *comprises your overall attitude.*

8. CHOICES—WHAT YOU DO

Poet, critic, and dictionary writer Samuel Johnson observed, "He who has so little knowledge of human nature as to seek happiness by changing anything but his own disposition will waste his life in fruitless efforts and multiply the grief which he purposes to remove." Most people want to change the world to improve their lives, but the world they need to change first is the one inside themselves. That is a choice—one that some are not willing to make.

In a *Peanuts* cartoon strip by Charles Schulz, Lucy says to her little brother Linus, "Boy, do I feel crabby."

"Maybe I can help you," Linus responds, always willing to be of assistance. "Why don't you just take my place here in front of the TV while I go and fix you a nice snack? Sometimes we all need a little pampering to help us feel better."

Linus returns with a sandwich, chocolate chip cookies, and a glass of milk.

"Now," he asks, "is there anything else I can get you? Is there anything I haven't thought of?"

Lucy takes the tray, saying, "Yes, there's one thing you haven't thought of." And then she screams, "I don't wanna feel better!"

Early in life, you don't have many choices. You don't choose where and when you are born. You don't choose your parents. You don't choose your race, your personality type, or your genetic makeup. You don't choose your health. Everything you are and nearly everything you do is not up to you. You must live with the conditions you find yourself in. As Voltaire would say, you start with the cards you're dealt.

But the longer you live, the more your life is shaped by your choices. You decide what you will eat. (This is one of the most common ways small children begin to assert their independence.) You decide what toys to play with. You decide whether you will do your homework or watch TV. You choose which friends to spend time with. You choose whether to finish high school, whether you will go to college, who you will marry, what you will do for a living. The longer you live, the more choices you make—and the more responsible you are for how your life is turning out.

Represented visually, it looks like this:

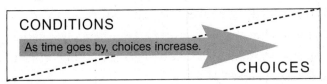

CONDITIONS

As time goes by, choices increase.

CHOICES

Obviously this graphic does not accurately represent every person's life. But in general, the longer we live, the less conditions dictate how we think and act, and the more our choices determine how we live. And one of those choices is our attitude.

I don't know what kind of circumstances you've had to face in your life. You may have had a really tough time. You may have faced extreme hardship or suffered terrible tragedies. However, your attitude is still your choice.

Perhaps the most remarkable story I've read in the face of horrible circumstances and personal tragedy is that of Viktor Frankl. Born in 1905, Frankl grew up in Vienna and showed an early interest in psychiatry. As a teenager, he corresponded with Sigmund Freud, and one paper he sent Freud so impressed him that the older man sent it to a professional journal, where it was later published.

Frankl became a successful medical doctor in Vienna at age twenty-five, but in 1942, four years after the Nazi invasion of Austria, he was rounded up along with other Austrian Jews and put in a concentration camp. While there, he experienced unspeakable horrors, and he lost his entire family: his pregnant wife, his parents, and his brother.

During the rest of World War II, Frankl was trapped in

concentration camps, including the notoriously brutal Auschwitz. Most of his fellow prisoners either were killed or gave up. Not Frankl. He not only maintained hope, but he helped others to find it. The key, he believed, was to find and hold on to meaning. Years later Frankl told Holcomb B. Noble in the *New York Times* that "the last of the human freedoms [is] to choose one's attitude in any given set of circumstances, to choose one's own way."[2]

Miraculously, Frankl survived his time in the concentration camps. And after the war, he was determined to use his experience to help others. He returned to school and earned a PhD. He developed Logotherapy, often called the "Third Viennese School of Psychotherapy." It is based on a person's will to find meaning and it is expressed, in part, by the attitude we take toward unavoidable suffering.[3]

Until he was eighty-five years old, Frankl taught in Vienna as a professor of neurology and psychiatry. He lectured at 209 universities on five continents. He received twenty-nine honorary doctorates and had more than 150 books published about him and his work in fifteen different languages. During the good years and the bad, his attitude was positive.

"Each man is questioned by life," Frankl once said,

TWO

What Your Attitude *Cannot* Do for You

I read an article in *USA Today* that pointed out issues that university professors and employers are having to address with many young men and women who are now entering adult life. These individuals were products of the self-esteem movement of the 1980s. Many have great attitudes about themselves. However, their high opinions of themselves and their abilities are often disconnected from reality.

Deborah Stipek, dean of education at Stanford University, says, "I often get students in graduate school doing doctorates who made straight A's all their lives, and the first time they get tough feedback, the kind you need to develop skills, [they react badly]. I have a box of Kleenex in my office because they haven't dealt with it before."[1]

Roy Baumeister, a psychology professor at Florida State University, has been studying self-esteem for more than thirty years. He thought it was going to be a key to helping people become successful, but it hasn't. "There is not nearly as much benefit as we hoped," he says. "It's been one of the biggest disappointments of my career."[2]

You cannot disconnect attitude from reality and expect success. I have to admit, I haven't always embraced this view. (A certain sign that we have grown intellectually is that over time our thoughts change.) If you had asked me about the importance of attitude twenty years ago, I'd have said, "Your attitude is the only difference between success and failure. You're only a dream away from success!" Back then, I thought that if you can believe it, you can achieve it, and all you had to do was make it happen.

> *You cannot disconnect attitude*
> *from reality and expect success.*

Today I recognize that, while those kinds of statements can motivate you, if you believe that a dream alone can bring success, you will be disappointed. Those statements simply aren't true. I know many people who have a great attitude yet aren't successful. Don't you? When all other things are equal, attitude can be the difference maker, but it alone does not make the difference.

For example, let's say two people apply for the same job. One has great skills and natural talent, ten years of experience, and an okay attitude. The other has a *great* attitude and no experience whatsoever. Who gets the job? Probably the one with the greater skills and experience. Why? Because a great attitude will not make up the gap. However, what if the two job candidates are roughly equal in skill and experience? In that case, the one with the better attitude wins hands down.

WHERE ATTITUDE *CANNOT* MAKE THE DIFFERENCE

Attitude is the difference maker. It is a plus; it gives an edge. It is an additive, but it is not a substitute. Here are some things that your attitude *cannot* make up for:

1. YOUR ATTITUDE CANNOT SUBSTITUTE FOR COMPETENCE

Some people seem to confuse confidence, which is a function of attitude, with competence, which is a function of ability. Or they believe that one can be substituted for the other. But the two are distinctly different. If you *think* you can do something, that's *confidence*. If you *can* do it, that's *competence*. Both are needed for success. A great attitude can help you *personally*. It can make you more content, more pleasant to be around, more likely to tackle difficult problems. But it cannot help you *positionally*. If you don't have competence in your favor, then you're going to be in trouble.

> *If you think you can do something, that's confidence. If you can do it, that's competence. Both are needed for success.*

To see the importance of competence, think about how much we desire it in others. When we hire employees, we certainly desire high competence. We want to find the best people we can. Management expert Peter Drucker once told my friend, Bill Hybels, that the team members he wanted to hire probably were neither unhappy nor unemployed. "If you find someone whose qualifications look good, but he or she is unhappy or unemployed, be very cautious," Drucker said. "The kind of people you're looking for are probably making huge contributions and setting records somewhere. They are probably happy and much loved by the people they work with. Go after that type. Go after proven competence."[3]

In leading and developing people for over thirty-five years, I have discovered that incompetence is a great distraction to people in an organization. When someone on the team is incapable of performing at the appropriate level—even someone with a great attitude—then the leader and the other team members become distracted from their main purpose. They end up spending a lot of time trying to get the incompetent person "on track."

In my book, *The 17 Indisputable Laws of Teamwork*, the Law of the Chain says, "The strength of the team is impacted by the weakest link." That is always true for any team. That problem often cannot be solved merely by adopting a positive attitude. However, it can change if the weak person gets on the ball quickly and develops competence.

2. YOUR ATTITUDE CANNOT SUBSTITUTE FOR EXPERIENCE

A fox, a wolf, and a bear went hunting, and each got a deer. A discussion followed about how they should divide the spoils.

The bear asked the wolf how he thought it should be done. The wolf answered, "That's simple. Each of us should get one deer." As soon as the wolf was done speaking, the bear ate him.

Then the bear asked how the fox proposed to divvy up the spoils. The fox offered his deer to the bear and suggested that the bear take the wolf's as well.

"Where did you get such wisdom?" asked the bear.

"From the wolf," replied the fox.

There are times when there is no adequate substitute for experience. The problem with experience, however, is that you rarely have it until after you need it.

The problem with experience is that you rarely have it until after you need it.

Experience is often a hard teacher because the test is given first and the lessons come afterward. That's probably why the old quote says, "When a person with experience meets a person with money, the person with experience will get the money, and the person with the money will get the experience!"

Back when I thought that attitude was everything, I tried to hire people with the best attitudes and figured I could get them up to speed in their skills. Now that I am older and more experienced, I realize that I had things backward. Now I hire primarily for skill and experience. Here's why: When it comes to talent and skill, a person can grow only a limited amount. On a scale from one to ten, most people can improve in a skill area only about two points. So, for example, if you are naturally a "6" as a leader, you may be able to grow to an "8" if you work at it. However, if you are a "2," you can work as hard as you want and you will never reach even average. The old saying of coaches is true: You can't get out what God didn't put in.

Attitude, however, is a different matter. There is no growth ceiling. Even a person with a "2" attitude can grow to become a "10." So even someone whose attitude isn't the best can turn that around.

On the day that I decided as a leader to hire only people with successful track records to key positions in my organization, my professional life changed. The entire team became more productive, and my organization began going to another level. That's not to say that I began hiring people with bad attitudes; I didn't. It wasn't an either/or decision. It was a both/and decision. Competence, experience, and positive attitude are a winning combination.

3. YOUR ATTITUDE CANNOT CHANGE THE FACTS

One of the interesting discoveries researchers have made about attitude is that it has an impact on people's health. A study performed by the University of Texas found that elderly people who had a positive attitude remained more physically hardy than those who were pessimistic.[4] That's really good news. But here's the bad news: No matter how good your attitude, it will not stop you from aging. That is just the way it is.

There are certain things in life that are simply facts, and your attitude will not change them. If you're an adult, your height is whatever it is. If you want to play center in the NBA and you're only 5 feet 4 inches tall, forget about it. The most positive attitude in the world isn't going to change that. Problems can be addressed and solved. Facts you just need to learn to live with. I love what poet Maya Angelou says about this, "If you don't like something, change it. If you can't change it, change your attitude. Don't complain."

4. YOUR ATTITUDE CANNOT SUBSTITUTE FOR PERSONAL GROWTH

Ernest Campbell, a former faculty member of the Union Theological Seminary in New York, told the story of a woman who bought a parrot at a local pet store because she was lonely. She took the bird home, but after a couple of days, she returned to the store to complain. "That parrot hasn't said a word yet!"

"Does it have a mirror?" the pet store owner asked. "Parrots like to be able to look at themselves in the mirror." So the lady bought a mirror and returned home.

The next day, she was back at the store because the bird still hadn't made a peep.

"What about a ladder?" the store owner asked. "Parrots enjoy walking up and down a ladder." So she bought a ladder and returned home.

She was back at the store the next day. Still the parrot hadn't said a thing.

"Does the parrot have a swing?" the owner asked. "Birds enjoy relaxing on a swing." She bought a swing and went home again.

The next day she returned to the store to tell the pet store owner that the bird had died.

"I'm terribly sorry to hear that," said the store owner. "Did the bird ever say anything before it died?"

"Yes," answered the lady. "It said, 'Don't they sell any food down there?'"

The lesson of the story, Campbell said, was that we buy mirrors by which to primp, ladders by which we try to climb higher, and swings upon which we seek pleasure, but we neglect food for our souls.

Musician Bruce Springsteen says, "A time comes when you need to stop waiting for the man you want to become and start being the man you want to be."[5] If you possess a good attitude, you have developed competence, and you have gained experience, what will keep you moving forward? Growth. Nothing can substitute for continual learning.

You need to feed your mind and soul to become the person you desire to be.

5. YOUR ATTITUDE WILL NOT STAY GOOD AUTOMATICALLY

I grew up in small-town rural Ohio, and there were plenty of farms nearby. I once heard a farmer say that the hardest thing about cows is that they never stay milked. A similar thing can be said about a good attitude. The hardest thing about having a good attitude is that it doesn't stay that way on its own.

If you're like most people, just getting to work in the morning is a test of your attitude. I live in the Atlanta area, which is notorious for its bad traffic. The latest report I read stated that we had the fourth worst traffic in the nation behind Los Angeles, San Francisco, and Washington, D.C. Not only that, but on any given day, the person in the vehicle next to you is likely to give you the "you're number one" signal, if you know what I mean. So every time I get in my car, I remind myself, *Today I am going to have a great attitude!*

That doesn't mean I always succeed. I have to remain sensitive to my personal attitude indicators. If I notice myself getting impatient—which is by far my greatest attitude challenge—I try to remind myself to have a good attitude. If I hear myself making cynical remarks, I check my attitude. If I find myself wanting to throw in the towel and stop developing people because they're not catching on quickly enough, I make an attitude correction. And my fail-safe attitude indicator is Margaret, my wife. If it's starting to get out of line, she tells me!

In my book *Today Matters*, one of the concepts I write about is that most people overrate decision making, and they underrate decision managing. It's pretty easy to say to yourself, *From now on, I'm going to have a great attitude*. It's much harder to actually follow through with it. That's why I believe one of the best things you can do for yourself is make the daily *management* of your attitude one of your objectives.

Believing that attitude is everything is really all-or-nothing thinking, and that's a problem. If you make attitude everything, then you are likely to end up with nothing. You cannot expect attitude to fix everything. Attitude is what it is: the difference maker.

There's a story of a young TV journalist that illustrates the limitations of a positive attitude. At age twenty-six, this young man was given an opportunity to anchor a network's evening newscast. He went head-to-head with Walter Cronkite, the most trusted news reporter of the time. The young man was sharp, he had grown up in the home of a newsman, he been a national-level news anchor in Canada prior to getting the job, and he had a good attitude. But it wasn't enough. In 1968, after three years, he stepped down from the job.

"I had the good sense to quit," he later said. But he

did not quit the news profession. What he needed was more experience and more skill. He became a foreign correspondent. For a decade, he took assignments that sent him to hot spots around the world. He went to Vietnam. He reported from the Middle East during the Yom Kippur War and the Lebanese civil war. He was at the Munich Olympics, where Palestinian terrorists murdered Israeli athletes.

In 1978, he returned to the anchor desk. This time he was a seasoned reporter. He was competent, he was experienced, and he had grown into the job. If you haven't already guessed, that reporter was Peter Jennings. When he worked the anchor desk the first time around, he had been called a "glamourcaster" or "anchorboy."[6] By the time he died in 2005, he was one of the most respected and watched reporters on television, having received the Edward R. Murrow Lifetime Achievement Award from Washington State University (2004), the Sol Taishoff Award for Excellence in Broadcast Journalism from the National Press Foundation (2000), fourteen National Emmy Awards, two George Foster Peabody Awards, several Overseas Press Club Awards, Harvard University's Goldsmith Career Award for Excellence in Journalism, the Radio and Television News Directors Paul White

Award (award chosen by the news directors of all three major networks), and the Order of Canada (2005).[7]

If attitude had been enough, then Jennings would have succeeded as ABC's anchor the first time around. Attitude by itself isn't enough. On the other hand, if he had not believed in himself and possessed an attitude of perseverance, he would not have succeeded either.

There are some things that attitude can do for you and others that it can't. To learn more about what it *can* do, turn the page, because that is the subject of the next chapter.

THREE

What Your Attitude *Can* Do for You

What usually separates the best from the rest? Have you ever thought about that? What separates the gold medalist from the silver medalist in the Olympics? What separates the successful entrepreneur from the one who doesn't make it? What makes it possible for one person to thrive after a debilitating accident while another gives up and dies? It's attitude.

Sure, every now and then there are people like Mozart or Lance Armstrong—those whose gifts are so extraordinary that they can achieve things the rest of us can only dream of. (But even they are assisted by the possession of extraordinary attitudes.) Most people at the top of their professions are comparable when it comes to talent. Gold and silver medals are usually separated by hundredths of seconds. Professional golfers win tournaments by a single stroke. As Denis Waitley said in *The Winner's Edge*, "The winner's edge is not in a gifted birth, a high IQ, or in talent. The winner's edge is all in the attitude, not aptitude. Attitude is the criterion for success. But you can't buy an attitude for a million dollars. Attitudes are not for sale."[1]

> *The greatest difference my difference maker can make is within me, not others.*

For years I have tried to live by the following statement: I cannot always choose what happens to me, but I can always choose what happens in me. Some things in life are beyond my control. Some things are within it. My attitude in the areas beyond my control *can* be the difference maker. My attitude in the areas that I do control *will* be the difference maker. In other words, the greatest difference my difference maker can make is within me, not others. That is why your attitude is your greatest asset or liability. It makes you or breaks you. It lifts you up or brings you down. A positive mental attitude will not let you do *everything*. But it can help you do *anything* better than you would if your attitude were negative.

WHAT ATTITUDE CAN DO FOR YOU

A positive attitude is an asset every day in nearly every way. It not only helps with little issues, but it also provides a positive framework from which a person can approach all of life. Here's what I mean:

1. YOUR ATTITUDE MAKES A DIFFERENCE IN YOUR APPROACH TO LIFE

As we neared the end of the twentieth century, much was written about the men and women who survived the Depression and fought World War II, the people Tom Brokaw called "the greatest generation." I recall reading a story about a woman of that generation who followed her husband during the war to a U.S. Army camp in the desert of southern California. The man had advised against it, thinking that she would be more comfortable back East with her family, but the young bride didn't want to be separated from her new husband.

The only living accommodation they could find was a run-down shack near a Native American village. The place was very basic. During the day, temperatures often reached 115 degrees. The wind, which blew constantly, felt like air from a furnace. And the dust made everything miserable.

The young woman found the days to be long and boring. Her only neighbors were Native Americans with whom she could find little in common. When her husband was sent into the desert for two weeks of maneuvers, she broke down. The living conditions and loneliness were too much for her. She wrote her mother to say that she wanted to come home.

A short time later, she received a reply from home. One of the things her mother told her was this:

Two men looked through prison bars;
One saw mud, the other saw stars.

As the young woman read the lines over and over, at first she felt ashamed. Then her resolve grew. She truly wanted to stay with her husband, so she made a decision. She would look for the stars.

The next day, she worked to make friends with her

neighbors. As she got to know them, she also asked them to teach her about their weaving and pottery. At first they were reluctant, but as they saw that her interest in them and their work was genuine, they became more open. The more the woman learned about the Native American culture and history, the more she wanted to know. Her perspective started changing. Even the desert began to look different to her. She began to appreciate its quiet beauty, its tough but beautiful plants, even the rocks and fossilized seashells she found as she explored it. She even began to write about her experiences there.

What had changed? Not the desert. Not the people who lived there. She had changed. Her attitude had transformed—and as a result, so did her outlook.

The happiest people in life don't necessarily *have* the best of everything. They just try to *make* the best of everything. They're like the person in a remote village going to a well every day to get water who says, "Every time I come to this well, I come away with my bucket full!" instead of, "I can't believe I have to keep coming back to this well to fill up my bucket!"

A person's attitude has a profound influence on his approach to life. Ask a coach before a big game whether his attitude and that of his players will make a difference in the outcome of the game. Ask a surgeon if the patient's attitude matters when she's trying to save that life in an emergency room. Ask a teacher if students' attitudes have an impact before they take a test.

One of the things I've learned is that life often gives you whatever you expect from it. If you expect bad things, those are what you get. If you expect good things, you often receive them. I don't know why it works that way, but it does. If you don't believe me, try it out. Give yourself thirty days in which you expect the best of everything: the best parking place, the best table in the restaurant, the best interaction with clients, the best treatment from service people. You'll be surprised by what you encounter, especially if you give your very best to others in every situation as well.

2. YOUR ATTITUDE MAKES A DIFFERENCE IN YOUR RELATIONSHIPS WITH PEOPLE

In August of 2005, I had the privilege to speak at the Willow Creek Leadership Summit. One of the people I met there was Colleen Barrett, president and corporate secretary for Southwest Airlines, who was also a speaker for the event. I was eager to talk to her because while other airlines have lost money and struggled to survive during the last several years, Southwest has succeeded and made a profit.

Colleen and I talked leadership. One of the things that she said the company was most proud of was their reputation for great customer service. When I asked her how they accomplished it, she told me that the company didn't rely on a lot of rules. There were, of course, FAA regulations that they complied with, and they had rules requiring that flight attendants always be on time for their assignments because their staffing is lean. But the company's emphasis is on creating the right kind of attitude among employees. Southwest's workers are empowered to evaluate situations and make decisions. And their focus is on people skills and the golden rule. Even when employees make mistakes, as long as they are attempting to see things from the customer's point of view and trying to give good service, they are supported.

To be successful, a person needs to be able to work well with others. That's why Theodore Roosevelt said, "The most important single ingredient in the formula for success is knowing how to get along with people."

Many factors come into play when it comes to skills working with people, but what makes or breaks that ability is a person's attitude. I recently wrote a book called *Winning with People* in which I describe twenty-five people principles that anyone can use to become better at building relationships and working with others. Many of those principles are attitude-based. Here are some examples:

- *The Lens Principle: Who we are determines how we see others.* Our perception of others depends more on our attitude than it does their characteristics. If we are positive, we see them as positive.

- *The Pain Principle: Hurting people hurt people and are easily hurt by them.* Our negative experiences and emotional baggage color our perception of others' actions. Normal interactions can cause us pain even when another person did nothing to inflict pain.

- *The Elevator Principle: We can lift people up or take them down in our relationships.* People possess a mind-set of either lifting or limiting others.

- *The Learning Principle: Each person we meet has the potential to teach us something.* Some people possess a teachable attitude, and they assume that they can learn something from everyone they meet.

Others look down on many people and assume that they have nothing to offer.

There are other attitude-based principles in the book, but you get the idea. When it comes to dealing with people, attitude makes a difference. If your track record of dealing with people isn't as good as you would like it to be, maybe you need to look at your attitude. While it's true that some people just seem to have a naturally winning way with others, even someone with limited natural people skills can learn to win with others if he decides to have a positive attitude toward people.

3. YOUR ATTITUDE MAKES A DIFFERENCE IN HOW YOU FACE CHALLENGES

It's said that when U.S. Marine Chesty Puller found himself surrounded by eight enemy divisions during the Korean War, his response was, "All right, they are on our left. They are on our right. They're in front of us. They're behind us—they can't get away from us this time!"

In life, obstacles, challenges, problems, and failures are inevitable. How are you going to handle them? Will you give up? Will you allow circumstances to make you miserable? Or are you going to try to make the best of things? Which path you choose depends on your attitude.

I once heard a lecturer say that no society has ever developed tough men during times of peace. The old adage is true: What doesn't kill you makes you stronger. Think back to the times in your life when you have grown the most. I'm willing to bet that you grew as the result of overcoming difficulties. The better your attitude, the more likely you will be to overcome difficulties, grow, and move forward.

You can see this pattern in the lives of great men and women:

Demosthenes, called the greatest orator of ancient Greece, possessed a speech impediment. Legend has it he overcame it by reciting verses with pebbles in his mouth and speaking over the roar of the waves at the seashore.

Martin Luther, father of the Reformation, made use of the time he was confined in the castle of Wartburg to translate the New Testament into German.

Composer *Ludwig van Beethoven* wrote his greatest symphonic masterpieces after he had become deaf.

John Bunyan wrote *Pilgrim's Progress* while in prison. *Daniel Defoe* also wrote while in prison, producing *Robinson Crusoe*.

Abraham Lincoln is considered by many to be the best of the United States' presidents, yet he probably would not have stood out as a great leader had he not led the country through the Civil War. Often difficult circumstances seem to be instrumental in the creation of great leaders and thinkers. But that is the case only when their attitudes are right.

I've been told that in the Chinese language two words are often combined to create another word with a very different meaning. For example, when the symbol for the word meaning *man* is combined with the symbol for the word meaning *woman*, the resulting word means *good*.

Possessing a positive attitude can have a similar effect. When a problem comes into contact with someone who has a positive attitude, the result is often something wonderful. Out of the turmoil that problems cause can emerge great statesmen, scientists, authors, or businesspeople. Every challenge has an opportunity. And every opportunity has a challenge. A person's attitude determines how she handles those.

4. YOUR ATTITUDE IS THE DIFFERENCE MAKER

When is attitude most important? When does it make the greatest difference? It's not during a sporting event or when business gets tough. It's when life itself is on the line. And in those instances, it truly is the difference maker.

When I was a pastor, I spent much time with people dealing with tragedies. I've visited with a lot of patients before surgery, and the ones who did the best afterward and recovered the most quickly were the people with the best attitudes. I've visited many nursing homes. The elderly people who thrive are the ones who are still positive about themselves and their situation. I heard from a nursing home official that the new patients who feel like they were forced into nursing homes and had no other options tended to give up and die sooner than those who saw it as just another phase of life to be met with positively.

Many people have written about the power of a positive attitude on health and fitness. Many medical personnel say they have seen a positive correlation between people's attitudes and their ability to recover from illnesses such as cancer. Dr. Ernest H. Rosenbaum and Isadora R. Rosenbaum say that these observations have led to new studies on attitude:

Researchers are now experimenting with methods of actively enlisting the mind in the body's combat with cancer. . . Some doctors and psychologists now believe that the proper attitude may even have a direct effect on cell function and consequently may be used to arrest, if not cure, cancer. This new field of scientific study, called psychoneuroimmunology, focuses on the effect that mental and emotional activity has on physical well-being, indicating that patients can play a much larger role in their recovery.[2]

Seeing a connection between people's thoughts and feelings and their health is nothing new. Rosenbaum points out, "We have known for over 2,000 years—from the writings of Plato and Galen—that there is a direct correlation between the mind, the body and one's health."[3] Poet John Milton wrote,

The mind is its own place, and it itself
Can make a heav'n of hell, a hell of heav'n.[4]

Your attitude has a profound influence on how you see the world—and thus on the way you live out your life.

Attitude is important. It is so important that it truly is the difference maker. It isn't everything, but it is one thing that can make a difference in your life. If you

FOUR

How to Make Your Attitude Your Greatest Asset

Former Yankee and Hall of Fame baseball player Yogi Berra has often been quoted as saying, "Life is like baseball; it's 95 percent mental, and the other half is physical." The former catcher and manager's math may not be perfect, but he does understand the power that thinking has on a person's ability to succeed. How many jobs do people lose every day because of attitude issues? How many times are others passed over for promotion because of the way they approach their job and other people? How many marriages fall apart? It would be impossible to calculate.

No one should ever lose a job, miss a promotion, or destroy a marriage because of a poor attitude. Why?

Because a person's attitude is not set; it is a choice. Pastor, professor, and author Chuck Swindoll says,

> Attitude, to me, is more important than education, than money, than circumstances, than failures, than successes, than what other people think or say or do. It is more important than appearance, giftedness, or skill. It will make or break a company . . . a church . . . a home. The remarkable thing is we have a choice every day regarding the attitude we embrace for that day. We cannot change our past . . . we cannot change the fact that people act in a certain way. We cannot change the inevitable. The only thing we can do is play on the one string we have, and that is our attitude. . . . I am convinced that life is 10 percent what happens to me and 90 percent how I react to it. And so it is with you. . . . [W]e are in charge of our attitudes.[1]

HOW TO CHOOSE THE RIGHT TRACK

1. TAKE RESPONSIBILITY FOR YOUR ATTITUDE

Singer Roberta Flack recalls, "My mother had only gone as far as the tenth grade, and my father had a third-grade education, but they both were very literate. They spoke well, and their values were high. They drummed into our heads that the situation you live in doesn't have to live in you." Our attitudes don't come from our circumstances or personal history. Attitude does not come from outside ourselves. It comes from within.

The first rule of winning is don't beat yourself. If your attitude isn't as good as it could be, and you fail to take personal responsibility for it, then you are beating yourself. However, if you look in the mirror and can with honesty say, "The attitude I possess is my responsibility and no one else's," then you're on your way.

2. Evaluate Your Present Attitude

To improve your attitude, you need to assess where you're starting from. This may take some time. And depending on how self-aware you are, it may even be difficult. The key is to try to look at yourself objectively, to separate yourself from your attitude. Your goal isn't to condemn yourself. It's to see yourself clearly so that you can make positive changes to the way you think. Here's how to proceed:

Identify problem feelings about yourself. Many times our feelings come into play long before we become consciously aware of them intellectually. So let's start with feelings. When do you feel most negative about yourself? Write down your answers.

Identify problem feelings related to others. Attitude issues often relate to other people. What causes you the greatest problems when dealing with others? Once again, write down your answers.

Identify problem thinking. We are the sum of our thoughts. And we cannot for any length of time behave in a way that is inconsistent with our thinking. So the question you must answer is this: What negative thoughts consistently control your mind? Write down your answers.

If you simply read through those questions without actually taking time to think through and write down your answers, then I want to encourage you to do so now. Why? Because you will not be able to change your attitude for the better unless you know what is currently impacting it for the worse. When professional loggers are floating logs down a river and they discover a log-jam, they climb a large tree near the river so that they can look over the problem and find the cause. What they're looking for is the key log that is creating the problem. Once they remove that, the river takes care of the rest. An inexperienced person could spend hours, days, even weeks moving around logs without results. Your attitude may be similar. You don't necessarily need to change *all* of your thinking—just the few items that are keeping a positive attitude from flowing in you.

3. DEVELOP THE DESIRE TO CHANGE

The desire to change is the key to growth in all areas of life. Ironically, most people desire improvement, yet at the same time they resist change. The problem is that you cannot get one without having the other. Change is possible, but only if you want it badly enough. As Fred Smith observed, "You are the way you are because that's the way you want to be. If you really wanted to be any different, you would be in the process of changing right now."

Comedian Jerry Lewis is reported to have said that the best wedding gift he received was a film of the entire wedding ceremony. Why was that his favorite gift? He said it was because when things got really bad in the marriage, he would go into a room by himself, close the door, run the film backwards, and walk out a free man!

Of course, change is never that easy. It takes lots of time, tremendous amounts of energy, perseverance, and—of course—desire. That's not a decision you make once and forget about. You need to cultivate that desire every day. It's said that when Earl Weaver, one-time manager of major league baseball's Baltimore Orioles, was unhappy with a call by an umpire, he used to charge out of the dugout and shout at him, "Are you gonna get any better, or is *this* it?" If you want to change your attitude, you need to ask yourself a similar question: Are you going to keep working and trying to get better, or is this as good as it gets?

4. CHANGE YOUR ATTITUDE BY CHANGING YOUR THOUGHTS

Norman Vincent Peale, author of *Power of the Plus Factor*, wrote that he once came across a tattoo studio in the twisted streets of Kowloon in Hong Kong. In the window were drawings of the hundreds of choices of tattoos available from the artist who worked there. One in particular really struck him. It said, "Born to lose."

Peale was appalled that anyone might actually ask to have that permanently written on his skin. He went inside and asked the Chinese artist, "Does anyone really have that terrible phrase 'Born to lose' tattooed on his body?"

"Yes, sometimes," the artist answered.

"But, I just can't believe anyone in his right mind would do that."

The artist tapped his forehead, and in broken English said, "Before tattoo on body, tattoo on mind."[2]

The human mind has a tremendous amount of power in our lives. That which holds our attention determines our actions. Because of that, where we are today is the result of the dominating thoughts in our minds. And the way we think determines what our attitudes are. But as I've already said, the good news is that you and I can change that. You can control your thoughts, and because of that, you can control your attitude.

Let's do an experiment that will show you what I mean. First, take a moment to think about the place where you live. No problem. You decided to think about it, and you did it. Okay, now I want you to think of something else. Imagine for a moment that the place where you live has burned to the ground, and everything in it is gone. What kind of emotional response did you have? Maybe you were sad because many irreplaceable things would have been lost in a fire. Maybe you were happy because your current living situation is terrible and a fresh start would do you good. The point is that your thinking prompts your emotion. That's key, and here's why:

> Major premise: We can control our thoughts.
> Minor premise: Our feelings come from our thoughts.
> Therefore: We can control our feelings by changing the way we think.

Why is that important? Because your attitude is your emotional approach to life. It's the framework through which you see events, other people, even yourself. That's why I believe the saying, "You are not what you think you are, but what you think . . . you are."

Sales trainer Brian Azar says, "Sales are not made or unmade inside the prospect's office. They are made or unmade inside you." In sales, if your attitude is positive and you believe you can help the prospect with your product or service, then the most difficult work is already done. It all depends on your thinking. The same thing works in other professions too.

> *You are not what you think you are,*
> *but what you think . . . you are.*

Once while flipping through a copy of ESPN's magazine, I saw an Adidas ad that arrested my attention. Here's what it said:

> Impossible is just a big word thrown around by small men who find it easier to live in the world they've been given than to explore the power they have to change it. Impossible is not a fact. It's an opinion. Impossible is not a declaration. It's a dare. Impossible is potential. Impossible is temporary. Impossible is nothing.[3]

Most of the great work in this world was done by men and women who didn't believe that what they were doing was impossible. Talent is certainly beneficial, but only the right attitude can release it to reach its potential.

5. Develop Good Habits

An annoyed middle-aged woman approached the clerk at her local bookstore. "Every time I come in here to buy a best seller, you're sold out," she criticized. "Why can't you people learn to stock your store more efficiently?"

"I'm so sorry," apologized the clerk. "What is the title of the book you want to purchase?"

"It's called *How to Remain Young and Beautiful*," the woman responded.

"Okay," replied the clerk. "I'll place an order for *How to Remain Young and Beautiful*, and I'll mark the order 'URGENT.'"

Much of what we do every day comes from habitual behaviors. Over the course of time, we have developed a way of approaching life. We treat people a particular way, as the lady in the bookstore did. If we desire to get different results out of life, then it's not enough to change only our thinking. We also need to change our habits. Why? Because if we don't we will revert back to our old thinking. In fact, some people recommend changing behavior first. Psychiatrist William Glasser says, "If you want to change attitudes, start with a change in behavior. In other words, begin to act the part, as well as you can, of the person you would rather be, the person you most want to become. Gradually, the old, fearful person will fade away."

I don't know which has to come first—the thinking or the habits. It's like the chicken or egg question. But I do know this: they are connected. Here's how I think it works:

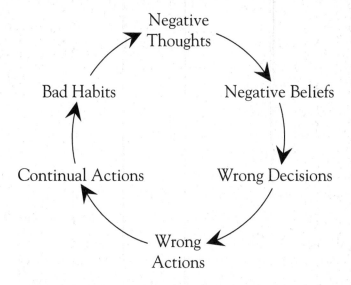

As you can see, negative thoughts lead to negative beliefs. Those beliefs become the basis of wrong decisions, which lead to wrong actions. When those wrong actions are continually repeated, we develop bad habits, which perpetuate a bad attitude. And that bad attitude prompts negative thoughts. It can be a vicious cycle. However, you can break the cycle by cultivating positive thoughts and developing good habits.

Fortunately, habits are not instincts. They are actions

or reactions that we have acquired over time. If you can pinpoint the original cause in your thinking that prompts a bad habit, you can change it.

6. MANAGE YOUR ATTITUDE DAILY

One of the most significant discoveries of my life was realizing that we often place too much emphasis on making decisions and too little on managing the decisions we've already made. This discovery was so significant to me that I wrote a book about it called *Today Matters*. The thesis of the book is that successful people make right decisions early and manage those decisions daily. You can make a decision to have a good attitude, but if you don't make plans to *manage* that decision every day, then you are likely to end up right back where you started. But here's the good news: *maintaining* the right attitude is easier than *regaining* the right attitude.

How do you do that? A Chinese proverb I came across gives insight: "Assume a cheerfulness you do not feel, and shortly you feel the cheerfulness you assumed." Or as editor and publisher Elbert Hubbard says, "Be pleasant until 10 a.m. and the rest of the day will take care of itself." When you get up in the morning, you need to remind yourself of the decision you've made to have a positive attitude. You need to manage your thinking and direct your actions so that they are consistent with your decision.

If you take responsibility for your attitude—recognizing that it can change how you live, managing it every day, and cultivating and developing positive thoughts and habits—then you can make your attitude your greatest asset. It can become the difference maker in your life, opening doors and helping you overcome great obstacles.

The Big Five
Attitude Obstacles

Before we move on to chapter five, I want to pause for a moment and talk to you about the Big Five Attitude Obstacles people face. In the first four chapters of this book, I've tried to give you a track to run on for creating and maintaining a positive attitude. However, to help you on your way, I need to give you something more. Maintaining a positive attitude while living life is a lot like running a race that includes hurdles. Some people expect life to be easy and smooth. When they encounter a hurdle, they become surprised, angry, or fearful. They don't think they should be expected to deal with such things. So they wait around for someone to remove the obstacle, they try to find a shortcut around it, or they simply give up and stop running. And during the process, their attitude gets worse and worse.

Successful people expect to face hurdles. They know that overcoming obstacles is a normal part of life, and they plan accordingly. They face their challenges instead of fearing them. They embrace the idea expressed by Walt Emerson, who said, "What lies behind us and what lies before us are tiny matters compared to what lies within us."

It's easy to have a positive attitude when the track is flat and everything is going your way. Your attitude really only becomes the difference maker when difficult challenges rise before you. In those moments, your attitude is sometimes the only difference between whether you press on or quit.

You already know about how to "run the race" with a good attitude. But there are especially difficult hurdles that everyone must overcome in the course of life. I call them the Big Five Attitude Obstacles: discouragement, change, problems, fear, and failure. I want to give you some extra help—some strategies for overcoming these five especially difficult challenges. When you can learn to deal with them in a positive way, you can face anything else life may have in store for you.

FIVE

Discouragement

When it comes to attitude obstacles, let's start with the one that's like the Trojan horse of ancient myth: discouragement. If you let discouragement get inside you, it can conquer you from the inside out, and it will prevent you from achieving the success you desire.

Don't misunderstand; everyone gets discouraged from time to time. Seldom does a day go by in my life without some discouraging thing happening to me. And then there are those times when you know it's going to be *one of those days*. I recently came across a humorous piece that tells about those days when it would be better to just stay in bed:

You know it's going to be a bad day when . . .

You turn on the morning news and it's showing
   emergency routes out of town.

The sun comes up in the west.

Your boss tells you not to bother taking off your coat.

You jump out of bed and you miss the floor.

The bird singing outside your bedroom window is a buzzard.

You wake up and your dentures are locked together.

Your car's horn gets stuck while you're following a group
   of Hell's Angels.

You put both contact lenses in the same eye.

You walk to work on a sunny morning and discover the
   back of your skirt is stuck in your panty hose.

You call to pick up your messages and are told it's none
   of your business.

Your tax return check bounces.

You put your bra on backwards and it fits better.

You step on the scale and it says "tilt."

You call suicide prevention, and they put you on hold.[1]

As I already mentioned, no one should expect life to
be smooth sailing. Sydney J. Harris says, "When I hear
somebody sigh, 'Life is hard,' I am always tempted to
ask, 'Compared to what?'" Think about the alternative!

If only life could become easier with every day of living! But that's not reality, is it? As you get older, truly some things get harder, but others also get easier. In every stage of life, there are good aspects and bad. The key is to focus on the good and learn to live with the bad. Of course, not everyone does that. In fact, I've found that there are really only two kinds of people in this world when it comes to dealing with discouragement: splatters and bouncers. When splatters hit rock bottom, they fall apart, and they stick to the bottom like glue. On the other hand, when bouncers hit bottom, they pull together and bounce back.

> *"Ninety percent of those who fail are not actually defeated. They simply quit."*—PAUL J. MEYER

Paul J. Meyer, founder of the Success Motivation Institute, says, "Ninety percent of those who fail are not actually defeated. They simply quit." That's what discouragement can do to you if you don't handle it the right way—it can cause you to quit. Since you *will* become discouraged at some point, the question is, Are you going to give up or get up?

DEALING EFFECTIVELY WITH DISCOURAGEMENT

The difference maker between splatters and bouncers is having the right attitude. If you believe in yourself, see discouragement as temporary, and handle it the right way, you can bounce back from nearly anything. Here are five steps you can take that will help you to deal effectively with discouragement:

1. GET THE RIGHT PERSPECTIVE

One of my favorite illustrations on perspective is something I came across years ago and like to use in conferences. It's in the form of a letter home from a girl at college:

Dear Mom,

Since I have been away at college, one full semester, I think it's time I bring you up to date as to what is going on. Shortly after I arrived at college, I got bored with dormitory life and stole fifty dollars from my roommate's purse. With the money, I rented a motorcycle, which I crashed into a telephone pole a few blocks from the dorm.

I broke my leg in the accident, but I was rescued by the young doctor who lives upstairs in the apartment house on the corner. He took me in, set my leg, nursed me back to health, and thanks to him, I'm up and around again.

We wanted to let you know that we're going to be married as soon as possible. Unfortunately, we're having some trouble with the blood test—they're not sure what the disease is, but it keeps showing up in the test. We hope to get that worked out quickly so that we'll be married before the baby arrives. Shortly thereafter we will all be home to live with you and Dad. And I just know you will learn to love the baby as much as you love me, even though the baby's dad is a different religion and wants us to convert. Please understand, the only reason we're coming back home to stay is that my husband-to-be got tossed out of medical school because he was too busy taking care of me to complete his work.

Really, Mom, I didn't steal any money or rent a motorcycle or hit a telephone pole or break my leg. I didn't meet a young doctor. There's no disease and I'm not expecting a baby. And I won't be coming home to live with you and Dad either. However, I *am* getting a D in algebra and an F in geology, and I wanted you to accept these grades in their proper perspective!

Take a good look at the whole picture. A man stopped to watch a Little League baseball game. He asked one of the players on the bench what the score was.

"We're behind eighteen to nothing," the boy answered.

"Well," remarked the man, "I have to say you sure don't look discouraged."

"Discouraged?" the boy said, puzzled. "Why should we be? We haven't come up to bat yet." For most people, the game of life is long, and we receive many opportunities to learn, to achieve, to serve, and to make amends for our mistakes. Take heart. No matter how dark things may seem at any given moment, there are always reasons to hope.

Take a short look at the problem. After the Civil War, former Confederate general Robert E. Lee visited the beautiful home of a wealthy Kentucky widow. After lunch, she invited Lee to join her on the porch. From there, she pointed to a once-majestic magnolia tree that had been badly burned by Northern artillery fire. The woman began to cry as she described the former magnificence of the tree that had shaded her home for generations. She expected Lee to condemn the Northern troops and sympathize with her loss. Finally, Lee said, "My dear madam, cut it down and forget it."[2]

Someone once said, "To hatch despair, just brood over your troubles."[3] Many people who experience setbacks ask *why*, but never move beyond that. Certainly you can't solve your problems by ignoring them. But you can't solve them by becoming fixated on them either. Once you recognize the problem, you need to focus your attention on solutions.

Take a close look at yourself. A man in his early sixties had just retired in Corgin, Kentucky. During his lifetime, he had worked as a farmer, streetcar conductor, soldier, railroad fireman, ferry boat operator, salesman, and service station operator. His latest venture had been cooking chicken. He had cooked from the time he was a boy of six, when his father died. He sold fried chicken at the gas station, and it had become so popular that he had moved his operation to a motel and restaurant across the street. But in the early 1950s, a planned interstate would bypass his operation. He sold off his operation, paid his bills, and faced living on a $105 a month Social Security check.

He wasn't ready to give up on life—not just yet. He took stock of his assets. He knew that others loved his chicken. In fact, in 1935 Kentucky's governor, Ruby Lafoon, had made the man an honorary Kentucky

Colonel. From then on, he had called himself Colonel Sanders and had dressed the part. Sanders decided to travel across the country cooking his chicken and making deals with restaurant owners. He would provide his blend of eleven herbs and spices, and the restaurant owners would pay him a royalty every time they sold chicken cooked with his recipe.

By 1964 Sanders had more than 600 franchised outlets for his chicken. That was the year he retired again. At the age of 74, he sold his interest in the Kentucky Fried Chicken restaurants for $2 million. But he didn't quit working. He became a marketing representative for the organization, which soon turned into a worldwide operation. He continued working for the restaurant chain, traveling 250,000 miles a year up until his death at age 90![4]

When you face discouragement, you can do one of two things, and the one you choose will color your perspective. You can look at others to place the blame, or you can look at yourself to discover your opportunities. The choice is yours.

Take a long look at successful people. One of the best ways to learn to have a positive attitude and achieve success is to study successful people and learn from them. That's what Napoleon Hill, author of *Think and Grow Rich*,[5] did. He studied the lives of more than five hundred successful people and got to know many of them personally. What he found was that they all shared one trait: persistence. The most successful people had often overcome the greatest obstacles. Their success hadn't come from their circumstances. It had come because of their attitudes.

Take a wide look at the possibilities. In most sets of negative circumstances lie positive possibilities. It's said that when Louis Waterman couldn't get a fountain pen to work when he needed a signature to close a deal, he went away and developed the fountain pen that bore his name. It became the premier writing instrument in the U.S. for fifty years.

When Alexander Fleming had a bunch of cultures he was working on at St. Mary's Hospital in London ruined by an open window, the resulting mold on some of them led him to the discovery of penicillin.

It is very likely that if you are facing something negative right now, there is an opportunity contained in it somewhere, somehow. It may not be easy to find. It may not outweigh the difficulty or lead to a major breakthrough as it did for Waterman and Fleming. But then again, it might. How will you ever know if you don't choose to adopt the right perspective and try to find it?

2. SEE THE RIGHT PEOPLE

Few things are better at helping someone overcome discouragement than spending time with the right person. Some people just lift you up. They help you to have hope or feel good about yourself. Poet Walt Whitman found such a person when he was a young man struggling to get anyone interested in his writing. In 1855 he published *Leaves of Grass*, a small volume of poetry. Because none of the big publishing houses would accept it, he paid neighborhood printers to produce 795 copies of it. It received little notice or acclaim from critics. And it didn't sell.

"He couldn't get rid of them," said Karen Karbiener, a Whitman professor at New York University. "The price was $2, then it went down to $1, then 50 cents."[6]

However, Whitman did receive a note of encouragement from someone. It said, "Dear Sir, I am not blind to the worth of the wonderful gift of *Leaves of Grass*. I find it the most extraordinary piece of wit and wisdom that America has yet contributed. I greet you at the beginning of a great career." Who was this encourager? None other than Ralph Waldo Emerson, the most respected literary figure of the day in America.

I am very fortunate because I grew up in the home of a lifter: my father, Melvin Maxwell. He really understands people and cares about them. When I was a teenager, he used to tell me, "Remember, everyone you come into contact with is fighting a battle." In his eighties and retired from pastoral ministry, he continues to be a lifter. When he moved to a retirement community several years ago, he started to connect with people in his community to encourage them and lend them a hand if they needed it. He had his golf cart and his cell phone, and he was always on the move. That first year, he asked me if I would be willing to speak to the couple of dozen people in his community if he got them together—just to encourage them—which I was glad to do.

Five years later, Dad has enlisted volunteers to help him and is active in thirty-seven retirement communities. This year when I spoke to his group, there were over 600 there! Why has Dad been so successful? Two reasons: first, he's a leader. He has always had the ability to make things happen. Second, he cares about people and lifts them up. If people feel discouraged, all they need to do is spend time with Dad to improve their attitude.

3. SAY THE RIGHT WORDS

A main source of discouragement is negative self-talk. D. Martyn Lloyd-Jones, once the greatest heart surgeon in England, says in his book *Spiritual Depression*, "Most of your unhappiness in life is due to the fact that you are listening to yourself rather than talking to yourself."[7] By that, I think he means that we often *passively* allow negative messages from our past to influence our thinking instead of *actively* telling ourselves good things that will help us to think more positively. For years I've used phrases such as these to help me:

- This too shall pass.
- Things could be worse.
- It's not what happens *to* me but what happens *in* me that matters most.
- Keep your chin up.
- Do it anyway.

You need to find your own phrases in a language that works for you. But be sure that the language is positively motivational, not negative or belittling. Nobody can motivate himself in a positive direction by continually using negative words.

4. Have the Right Expectations

Clergyman J. Wallace Hamilton once observed, "Every person's life is a diary in which he or she means to write one story and is forced to write yet another." Haven't you found that to be true? I know I have. Here's the good news: the story you write can actually be *better* than the one you envisioned, but you need to have the right expectations. You have to remain flexible, and you can't expect everything to go perfectly.

Lawrence R. Burns, a psychology professor at Grand Valley State University in Allendale, Michigan, makes the distinction between negative and positive perfectionists. He says that negative perfectionists are "concerned with trying to impress" and as a result are often depressed, anxious, and obsessed with their flaws. Positive perfectionists, on the other hand, set realistic goals and forgive themselves when they fall short. And Burns says it is possible for a person to shift from one to the other. The key is to focus on what you can achieve, not what you can't.[8]

5. MAKE THE RIGHT DECISIONS

Do you ever feel worn out by the end of the day? Maybe it's because you are making decisions that cause you to expend your energy the wrong way. Take a look at the following list of activities reputed to have come from the Southern California Medical Association and the number of calories each burns to see if that may be the problem:

Activity	Calories
Beating around the bush	75
Jogging your memory	125
Jumping to conclusions	100
Climbing the wall	150
Swallowing your pride	150
Passing the buck	25
Beating your own drum	100
Throwing your weight around	300
Turning the other cheek	75
Dragging your heels	100
Throwing in the towel	200[9]

Seriously, the decisions you make and how you make them have a huge impact on your outlook. First, it's important always to do the right thing. Few things increase discouragement the way regret or a guilty conscience can. It's not easy to apologize, admit your faults, forgive, subdue your temper, shoulder a deserved blame, or start over. But making the decision to do these things when they're called for always pays off. Each of us needs to be willing to look at life realistically, see ourselves as we are, and come to terms with what's true.

Second, the timing of the decision is also important. Many people make decisions when things aren't going well. They look for relief in the despair of the valley instead of waiting for the clarity that comes from being on the mountaintop. Why? Because it takes a lot of effort to get to the mountaintop. And when you're experiencing the darkness of the valley, it's always tempting to make changes that you hope will relieve the discomfort.

Robert Schuller, founder of the Crystal Cathedral in Orange, California, calls this the Peak to Peak Principle. It can be represented visually like this:

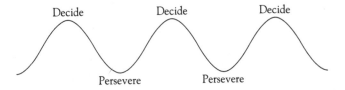

When you are on top of the proverbial mountain, that is the time to make decisions. Here's why:

You can see your situation more clearly.

You are moving to something, not just from something.

You leave those around you in a better position.

You decide using positive data, not negative.

You are more likely to move from peak to peak instead of valley to valley.

On the other hand, when you're in the valley, the most important thing you can do is persevere. If you keep fighting, you're likely to get your second wind, just as distance runners do. And it's said that only when runners are exhausted enough to reach that place do they find out what they can truly accomplish. If you keep persevering while you are in the valley, not only will you likely make it to higher ground where you can make better decisions, but you will also have developed character, which will serve you well throughout life.

Many years ago I came across the poetry of Helen Steiner Rice, and it intrigued me because it seemed to be characterized by hope in the midst of pain or sorrow. When I learned about her story, it made sense to me.

Helen was born in 1900 and grew up on the shores of Lake Erie. Her dream was to study law, but her plans to attend Wesleyan College had to be set aside when her father died during the influenza epidemic of 1918. Instead, she ended up taking a job with an electrical utility company.

In 1928 Helen met a young banker named Franklin Rice. Soon they were married. But their happiness together was short-lived. In the wake of the stock market crash of 1929, Franklin committed suicide.

Helen went back to work, this time taking a job editing greeting cards. For twenty years she worked in the industry, with some of her poems being published by the Gibson Card Company. And she worked and maintained a grateful attitude despite suffering a painful degenerative disease.

Then one day one of her cards was read on *The Lawrence Welk Show*, and her life suddenly changed. People clamored for her poetry. Since then, people have bought more than seven million books of her writing.

She died in 1981, but one of the poems she published before her death describes a discovery she made when facing dark times. The poem is called "The Bend in the Road," and it ends this way:

And together we stand at life's crossroads
And view what we think is the end,
But God has a much bigger vision
And He tells us it's only a bend.

For the road goes on and is smoother,
And the pause in the song is a rest.
And the part that's unsung and unfinished
Is the sweetest and richest and best.

So rest and relax and grow stronger.
Let go and let God share your load,
Your work is not finished or ended,
You've just come to a bend in the road.

If you can maintain that perspective, you can overcome discouragement and move beyond it. No one need
be held captive to it. Embrace the difference maker and
it will make the difference in you.

SIX

Change

On August 3, 1492, Columbus set sail from Palos in southern Spain in search of a western route to Asia. He was convinced that the world was round, despite the belief by nearly everyone else in Europe that it was flat. Most people believed that a ship sailing due west would fall off the edge of the earth!

Columbus didn't find the route he sought, but he did confirm his suspicions that the earth was a sphere. And after months of exploration and the loss of one ship, he returned to Palos on March 15, 1493—a hero. And in a matter of months, the perspective of everyone in Europe concerning the earth changed drastically. It caused a quick and transforming revolution of the world. Right? Not exactly.

Columbus was considered a hero for returning from his venture. And he was credited with discovering new lands. But people didn't change their minds about the earth. As David Bayles and Ted Orland, authors of *Art and Fear*, state, when Columbus returned from the New World and proclaimed the earth was round, almost everyone else went right on believing the earth was flat. Then they died, and the next generation grew up believing the world was round. That's how people change their minds.[1]

Everyone resists change. For many years, I thought leaders liked change and everyone else didn't. As a visionary leader, I always felt that I was drawing reluctant followers into the future. But I finally realized that leaders don't like change any more than followers do— unless, of course, it's their idea!

WHY DO PEOPLE RESIST CHANGE?

Change is hard for everyone. Novelist Mark Twain said, "The only person who likes change is a wet baby." Truly, change is one of the greatest attitude obstacles you will ever face. Why is that? After all, doesn't progress require change? And doesn't growth? We can't move forward and stay the same at the same time. Yet we resist change. Why? There are several reasons:

1. People Resist Change Because of Personal Loss

Whenever change is imminent, the first question that pops into people's minds is how the change will affect them. For example, imagine that a coworker came up to you today and said, "I just heard that the boss is laying off some people today." Was your first thought, *I wonder what market conditions precipitated such a decision?* Or was it, *Boy, I bet the boss feels bad about having to do that?* Or, *I wonder how that will impact the bottom line of the company?* No, chances are your first thought was, *Am I at risk?* That's just human nature. In the moments that we face change, we can suddenly feel alone and vulnerable.

Optimistic people will more quickly see the good in most changes, and they may try to encourage you by saying something such as, "It's okay. This change is for the better." But the truth is that there is loss even in positive changes. Ralph Waldo Emerson said, "For everything you gain, you lose something." In life, there are wins and losses. Even when change is good, we will give up things that are important to us.

Back in 1996 when I decided to relocate my companies from San Diego to Atlanta, it was a win for the organization. It was the right move for many reasons. Yet it meant leaving many good friends, the place that felt like home, and the best weather in the world. It was a win that contained losses. As poet and literary critic Paul Valéry observed, "Every beginning is a consequence. Every beginning ends something." If not seen correctly, that can be disheartening.

> *"Every beginning is a consequence. Every beginning ends something."*—PAUL VALÉRY

2. PEOPLE RESIST CHANGE BECAUSE OF FEAR OF THE UNKNOWN

I love a story that my friend Zig Ziglar tells: A man from out in the sticks won a bass fiddle in a drawing. He took it home and looked at the beginning music book that had come with it. Unfortunately, the book had been damaged and the only part that survived intact was one page showing the left hand in one position on the strings and the right hand drawing the bow. So he carefully placed his fingers and drew the bow back and forth across the stings, producing an awful sound. And though it was the only sound he could make, he practiced every day. This of course drove his wife crazy.

Then one day his wife went to a concert, and by chance her seat was not very far from the bass fiddle player in the orchestra. She was delighted by the sound *this* player produced with his instrument, and she watched as his fingers traveled up and down the instrument's fret board and the bow moved in various rhythms. It was beautiful.

As she traveled home she decided that she wanted to communicate to old Johnny One Note the potential of his instrument, but she also knew that he was easily upset. As it happened, the man was practicing when she arrived at home.

"Honey," she said, "may I ask you a question?"

"Sure," he answered, continuing to saw at the strings.

"At the concert I noticed that the bass fiddle player kept moving his left hand up and down and left and right while his right hand moved slowly on some occasions and fast on others." She said this gently, not wanting to upset him. "I'm just curious why he moves his hands so much and does so many things while you keep your hands in exactly the same spot all the time."

"That's easy," he answered. "That old boy's still lookin' for his place, and I done found mine!"

People often avoid change because they worry about the unknown. You've probably heard the quote, "The only thing we have to fear is fear itself." Deadpan comedian Pat Paulson said, "The only thing we have to fear is fear itself—and possibly the bogeyman." Ironically, it's the "bogeyman" who often causes us to resist change. It's what we *don't* know that makes us afraid.

> *"The only thing we have to fear is fear itself—and possibly the bogeyman."*—PAT PAULSON

People often cling to what they know, even if they are not satisfied with it. Fear holds them back, yet the only way to overcome the fear is to go out and do the very thing they fear to do.

Fear can be such a difficult problem that I have dedicated an entire section of this book to it, so I don't need to go into it much further here. But I will say this: All the things you love were once unknown to you. Don't be afraid to keep trying something new.

3. PEOPLE RESIST CHANGE BECAUSE THE TIMING COULD BE WRONG

Law 19 in *The 21 Irrefutable Laws of Leadership* states, "When to lead is as important as what to do and where to go." What happens when you try to make a change at the wrong time? For that matter, when is the right time to make changes? From a leadership point of view, there actually are better times for change than others. I developed the following checklist to help me navigate the process:

A Checklist for Change
○ Will this benefit the followers?
○ Is this change compatible with the purpose of the organization?
○ Is this change specific and clear?
○ Are the top 20 percent (the influencers) in favor of this change?
○ Is it possible to test this change before making a total commitment to it?

- o Are physical, financial, and human resources available to make this change?
- o Is this change reversible?
- o Is this change the next obvious step?
- o Does this change have both short- and long-range benefits?
- o Is the leadership capable of bringing about this change?
- o Does everything else indicate the timing is right?

Before implementing a big change, I run through this checklist and answer each question with a yes or no. If too many questions have a no by them, then I conclude that the timing may not be right.

4. PEOPLE RESIST CHANGE BECAUSE IT FEELS AWKWARD

When was the last time you did something for the first time? Can you name something specific? It has to be something really new. Seeing a new movie doesn't count —because you've seen a movie before. It needs to be a real first. If you can't remember, then you might be in trouble.

I want you to do an experiment. Don't get annoyed by it; just trust me. First, I want you to set this book down and clasp your hands together, palms together with your fingers interlocked. Try it.

If I asked you to do this ten times—which I won't—you will lock your fingers together the same way every time, with one thumb over the other. Now I want you to try something. Clasp your hands together again, but *this* time I want you to interlock your fingers in such a way that the *other* thumb is on top. Try it.

Didn't that feel weird? That's what change does—it makes you feel awkward. It isn't wrong; it's just different, and that takes us out of our comfort zone.

5. PEOPLE RESIST CHANGE BECAUSE OF TRADITION

Cambridge University professor F. M. Cornford said, "Nothing is ever done until everyone is convinced that it ought to be done and has been convinced for so long that it is now time to do something else." Many people cling to tradition. The assumption is that if something is tradition, it must be a better way. But that's not necessarily so. Here's a riddle that shows what I mean: How many traditionalists does it take to change a light bulb? The answer is four: one to change it and three to talk about how wonderful the old bulb was.

If a tradition connects you to other people or to your

personal history, it can be a good thing. If it doesn't, then it may be time to try something else.

PREPARATION POINTS FOR SUCCESSFUL CHANGE

The keys to dealing with change successfully are having a good attitude toward it and being prepared to meet it. The following ideas can help you to do those things:

1. CHANGE WILL HAPPEN WHETHER YOU LIKE IT OR NOT

It's said that a duke of Cambridge once said, "Any change at any time for any reason is to be deplored." I feel sorry for people like him. They have a hard time dealing with reality and experience a difficult life. Change is unavoidable. The only thing certain about tomorrow is that it will be different from today. If you doubt that, consider this: My grandfather had a farm, my parents had a garden, and I've got a can opener! It's a different world than it was twenty years ago, and it will be different in another twenty. But the good news is that the world changes so fast that you couldn't stay wrong all the time if you tried!

2. WITHOUT CHANGE THERE CAN BE NO IMPROVEMENT

I am not a proponent of change for its own sake. That's often a characteristic of restlessness and can be a symptom of personal inner conflict. Honestly, change can represent both possible opportunities and potential losses. Even though all progress brings change, not all change brings progress. But as leadership expert Max DePree observed, "We cannot become what we need by remaining what we are." If you desire growth, then you must embrace change.

General Douglas MacArthur stated, "Life is a lively process of becoming. If you haven't added to your interests within the past year, if you are thinking the same old thoughts, relating the same personal experiences, having the same predictable reactions, *rigor mortis* of the personality has set in." If you don't change the direction you are going, then you're likely to end up where you're heading. When you want something you've never had, then you have to do something you've never done. That means changing.

3. MAKE A COMMITMENT TO PAY THE PRICE FOR CHANGE

American dramatist and screenwriter Sidney Howard remarked, "One half of knowing what you want is

knowing what you must give up before you get it."
Change always costs you something, if not monetarily,
then in time, energy, and creativity. In fact, if change
doesn't cost you anything, then it isn't real change!

As you consider how to make the changes needed to
improve and grow, it is important to measure the cost of
change compared to the cost of the status quo. You have
to do your homework. That often makes the difference
between

change = growth
and
change = grief.

What will the changes you desire really cost you?

*If change doesn't cost you anything,
then it isn't real change.*

Management expert Tom Peters gives a perspective
on this. He suggests, "Don't rock the boat. Sink it and
start over." If you desire to be creative and do something

really innovative, that's sometimes what it takes. You must destroy the old to create something new. You cannot allow yourself to be paralyzed by the idea of change.

4. CHANGE MUST HAPPEN WITHIN YOU BEFORE IT CAN HAPPEN AROUND YOU

I love the *Peanuts* comic strip by Charles Schulz in which Lucy says to Charlie Brown, "I would like to change the world."

"Where would you start?" Charlie Brown asks her.

Lucy's simple reply: "I would start with you."

I hate to say it, but our attitude is probably a lot more like Lucy's than we would care to admit. If we don't like something, we desire change—for everyone other than us! We are resistant to change.

Novelist Frances Hodgson Burnett wrote,

At first people refuse to believe that a strange new thing can be done,
and then they begin to hope it can be done,
then they see it can be done—
then it is done and all the world wonders why it was not done centuries ago.[2]

Artist Andy Warhol observed, "They always say that time changes things, but you actually have to change them yourself." The truth is that any change that occurs in the world always begins first with change *within* an individual. That's why playwright George Bernard Shaw said, "Progress is impossible without change; and those who cannot change their minds cannot change anything."

> *"They always say that time changes things, but you actually have to change them yourself."*—ANDY WARHOL

The good news is that once you dedicate yourself to growth and develop a lifestyle of planned improvement from the inside out, it becomes normal to you. And you notice when you're not making the progress you have come to expect. It is said that pianist Arthur Rubenstein refused to listen to recordings made of songs he had played. Even only a few months after he had completed them, he was dissatisfied with the playing he heard. Why? Because he had grown and changed, but the recordings had not.

5. DECIDE WHAT YOU ARE NOT WILLING TO CHANGE

I have to admit that I'm a personal growth fanatic. There are few things I enjoy more than learning something new. My father got me started when I was a kid. He actually paid me to read books that would help me learn and grow. Now I'm in my late fifties, and I still love it when I can see myself improving in an area I've targeted for growth. But as much as I am dedicated to progress, there are some things that I'm not willing to change—no matter what—such as my faith and my values. I'd rather die than forfeit my faith in God or my commitment to integrity, family, generosity, and belief in people. Some things are not worth compromising at any price.

I want to encourage you to think about the nonnegotiables in your life. What are you willing to live and die for? Write down the things you will hold on to no matter what, and take some time to explain why. Once you do that, then *everything* else should be open to change.

6. REMEMBER, IT'S NEVER TOO LATE TO CHANGE

I already mentioned that I am in my late fifties. The older I get, the more I meet people my age who express regret for the way they've lived their lives. Sometimes the regret is for things they've done, but more often it is for things they *didn't* do but felt that they should have. If they ask for my advice, I quote one of my favorite sayings:

Though you cannot go back
And make a brand-new start, my friend.
Anyone can start from now
And make a brand-new end.

It's never too late to change. As the Turkish proverb says, "No matter how far you have gone on a wrong road, turn back."

My friend Dick Biggs, a speaker and author, delivers a program called "The Headache of Changing or the Headache of Not Changing." I just love that title because it really describes the dilemma we all feel when faced with the prospect of change. A positive thinker with a good attitude, Dick has also written a poem on the subject. He has graciously allowed me to share it with you.

Will I Master Change, or Will Change Master Me?
by Dick Biggs

Life's turning points are as sure as the tide
Just a matter of when, so why not decide?

To embrace these transitions as ways to grow
'Tis folly to ignore what you already know.

Make a vow to adapt to the crises of life
There's no reason to suffer more stress or strife.
Quite often change becomes a blessing in time
While making you wiser in pursuit of your prime.
No change is impossible, no one is exempt
You can step out in faith or shrug with contempt.
Life comes in cycles, no two are the same
To claim nothing's new is a naïve game.

Some change is impractical, some things must endure
You need worthwhile values, so profound and pure.
Plus a noble purpose to guide you each day
And give life meaning as you forge your way.

But *most* things do change, it's a natural law
You can believe this is truth or stand there in awe.
It may be uncomfortable, it may cause pain—
Won't a regretful heart be a greater strain?

With *every* change, there's an outcome to bear
So accept the challenge, for life's seldom fair.

Be willing to risk and you're bound to find
More courage and strength from a positive mind.

Be bold, be daring, be receptive to change
For most things are better when you rearrange.
Get out of the rut, seek a new vitality
Move beyond the old to a fresh reality.

Ah, life has turning points, they won't disappear
Rise up to greet them and conquer your fear.
The choice is simple, it's as clear as can be:
Will I master change or will change master me?

In the end, that is really the question. You can allow change to *get* the best of you, or you can harness change and let it help *make* the best of you. To do that, you need to have a positive attitude about it. You need to keep relying on the difference maker.

HOW YOUR ATTITUDE CAN BE THE DIFFERENCE MAKER CONCERNING CHANGE

Think about a change you are currently resisting. It can be a change you feel prompted to make or are currently being asked to make by others. Define the change as clearly as you can here:

Next, write down all the benefits of the change:

Now consider why you are resisting the change. Answer yes or no to each of the following questions:

Yes	No	Question
___	___	1. Are you uncertain of what will happen as a result of the change?
___	___	2. Are you concerned that the timing is wrong?
___	___	3. Does the change violate tradition?
___	___	4. Will it create some kind of loss to you personally?
___	___	5. Will the change make you feel awkward?

If you answered yes to question 1 or 2, use the Checklist for Change from earlier in the chapter to explore the issues at greater depth.

If you answered yes to question 3, explore why you are clinging to the tradition. What real value does the tradition have to you, to others in the organization, or to the people you serve? Write that down. Now weigh that value against the benefits you listed previously.

If you answered yes to question 4 or 5, spend some time thinking about how improvement can come only with change. And think about your motives. Are you putting yourself ahead of the organization or the people you serve? Keeping in mind the value of the change can sometimes help a person to make difficult transitions.

No matter how you answered the questions, keep in mind that for positive change to occur . . .

1. You must make a commitment to pay the price for change;
2. Change must happen within you before it can happen around you; and
3. It's never too late to change.

SEVEN

Problems

Recently I was flipping through a magazine when an ad for a company called Accenture caught my eye. The page showed golfer Tiger Woods on a golf green leaning down to line up a putt. He is holding his putter in his left hand, and he has just set down his ball. His gaze is highly focused—burningly intense—on the hole. At the top of the page are the words, "Waiting for ideal conditions is rarely an option." Only after reading those words did I realize that in the foreground of the picture is a man in heavy rain gear squeegeeing a lot of water off the green in preparation for the putt. Evidently, Woods is plying his craft in the midst of a rainstorm, yet it doesn't seem to be fazing him a bit. Right below the image of Woods it says, "Go on. Be a Tiger."

A PERSPECTIVE ON PROBLEMS

That's the way things are for all of us, isn't it? We try to get things done—whether work, play, family interaction, or something else—and we find ourselves having to do so in the midst of storms. We simply can't avoid them. Here's what I mean:

1. PROBLEMS ARE EVERYWHERE, AND EVERYBODY HAS SOME

A man living in New York City got up early one morning, and before he was able to leave home for the day, he received four long-distance calls from clients who had problems—every one of whom wanted him to hop on a plane to try to fix them. He finally finished getting dressed and went out to the kitchen where he received two more calls, this time from local clients. He told his wife he was skipping breakfast, and went down and hailed a cab.

"All right, let's get going," he hollered as he jumped in.

"Where do you want me to take you?" asked the cabbie.

"I don't care," replied the man. "I've got problems everywhere."

Do you ever have days that feel like that? Everywhere you turn you see more problems. No one is exempt from the difficulties of life. Having money doesn't protect people from having problems. Neither does social standing, talent, or a good job. In fact, Malcolm Forbes observed, "If you have a job without aggravations, you don't have a job."

Pick any person living or dead, and, if you look, you will see that he had problems.

Problems are simply inescapable. If you're a human being and you're breathing, you will have problems.

2. OUR PERSPECTIVE ON THE PROBLEM, NOT THE PROBLEM ITSELF, USUALLY DETERMINES OUR SUCCESS OR FAILURE

Alfred Armand Montapert said, "The majority see the obstacles; the few see the objectives; history records the successes of the latter, while oblivion is the reward of the former." People's perspectives make a huge difference in how they approach their problems. Take a look at the differences between the wrong and right approaches:

A Wrong Perspective	A Right Perspective
Problems are unsolvable	Problems are solvable
Problems are permanent	Problems are temporary
Problems are *not* normal	Problems are a normal part of life
Problems make us bitter	Problems make us better
Problems control us	Problems challenge us
Problems stop us	Problems stretch us

One of the reasons that problem solving is so difficult is that we are often too close to the problems to truly understand them. Novelist John Galsworthy observed, "Idealism increases in direct proportion to one's distance from the problem." By standing back (either literally or figuratively), you can often get a better perspective on a problem. And that better perspective will not only help you to feel better about it, but will also help you to solve it more easily.

3. THERE IS A DIFFERENCE BETWEEN PROBLEM SPOTTING AND PROBLEM SOLVING

Cartoonist Ashleigh Brilliant remarked, "I don't have any solutions, but I certainly admire the problem." Isn't that the way some people operate? They're very quick to find any kind of problem and point it out. For example, look at the following remarks, which were taken from actual registration sheets and comment cards returned to the staff in 1996 at the Bridger Wilderness Area in Wyoming:

○ Trails need to be wider so people can walk holding hands.

○ Trails need to be reconstructed. Please avoid building trails that go uphill.

○ Too many bugs and leeches and spiders and spiderwebs. Please spray the wilderness to rid the area of these pests.

○ Please pave the trails so they can be plowed of snow during the winter.

○ Chairlifts need to be in some places so that we can get to wonderful views without having to hike to them.

○ The coyotes made too much noise last night and kept me awake. Please eradicate these annoying animals.

○ A small deer came into my camp and stole my jar of pickles. Is there a way I can get reimbursed?

○ Reflectors need to be placed on trees every 50 feet so people can hike at night with flashlights.

- ○ Escalators would help on steep hill sections.
- ○ A McDonald's would be nice at the trailhead.
- ○ The places where trails do not exist are not well marked.
- ○ Too many rocks in the mountains.[1]

To become someone who overcomes problems, you need to become a problem solver.

4. THE SIZE OF THE PERSON IS MORE IMPORTANT THAN THE SIZE OF THE PROBLEM

You can tell the caliber of a person by the amount of opposition it takes to discourage him. Orison Swett Marden, founder of *Success* magazine, observed, "Obstacles will look large or small to you according to whether you are large or small." Big people overcome big obstacles.

There's a world of difference between a person who has a big problem and a person who makes a problem big. It's said that legal immigrants in the United States are four times as likely to become millionaires as native-born Americans. They do this despite the additional obstacles they often face, such as language differences, culture shock, separation from family, and isolation.

Joke writer Robert Orben says that he once saw an ad

in a show business paper that read, "Lion tamer—wants tamer lion." Obviously, that circus performer had room for growth. Instead of working to increase himself, he desired to shrink the problem.

5. PROBLEMS, RESPONDED TO CORRECTLY, CAN ACTUALLY ADVANCE US FORWARD

A young woman was complaining to her father about her problems and how difficult her life was.

"Come with me," he said. "I want to show you something." He took her into the kitchen where he put three pots of water on the stove to heat. Meanwhile, he cut up some carrots and put them into the first pot to boil. Into the simmering water in the second pot he put two eggs. In the third pot he poured some ground coffee. After a few minutes, he strained the carrots into one bowl, peeled the eggs and put them into another, and into a cup he poured the strained coffee. Then he placed them before his daughter.

"What's all this supposed to mean?" she asked somewhat impatiently.

"Each of these items can teach us something about the way we handle adversity," he answered. "The carrots started out hard, but the boiling water turned them mushy. The eggs went into the water fragile but came out hard and rubbery. The coffee, on the other hand, changed the water into something better."

"Sweetheart," he said, "you can choose how you will respond to your problems. You can let them make you weak. You can let them make you hard. Or you can use them to create something beneficial. It's all up to you."

For decades, Victor and Mildred Goertzel have studied the lives of famous people who achieved success. They first published their findings in 1962 in *Cradles of Eminence*, and have since revised and updated it. What did they find to be the greatest commonality between the successful people they studied? Would it surprise you to know that most of them had huge obstacles to overcome? The problems they faced—some physical, some emotional, and some financial—prompted them to achieve. Many likely would not have been driven to succeed without the problems they overcame.

PRINCIPLES FOR HANDLING PROBLEMS

Recognizing problems for what they are—temporary tests of your resolve and ability—won't do you much good if you don't know how to overcome the problems and move forward. After all, the best way to escape a problem is to solve it. Here is some advice concerning how:

1. Define What a Real Problem Is

Philosopher Abraham Kaplan makes a distinction between problems and predicaments. A problem is something you can do something about. If you can't do something about it, then it's not a problem. It's a predicament. That means it's something that must be coped with, endured.

> *A problem is something you can do something about. If you can't do something about it, then it's not a problem. It's a predicament.*

When people treat a predicament as a problem, they can become frustrated, angry, or depressed. They waste energy. They make bad decisions. And when people treat problems as predicaments, they often settle, give up, or see themselves as victims.

Let me give you a few examples to help you get a handle on what I mean. If you are married, chances are that if you are a morning person, your spouse is a night person (or vice versa). That is a predicament. You can't change that. You can't change the way people are wired internally. If you try to, you and your spouse will experience lots of conflict, and there will be no resolution. However, your difficulty in finding ways to spend time together because of your different bents *is* a problem, and it *can* be solved.

Here is another example. Let's say you go to work one day and find out that the company you work for is going out of business. It's done, and that means your job is gone. That is a predicament—unless you are in a position financially to buy the business. Assuming that you're not, then what are you going to do? Are you going to waste energy complaining about losing your job or trying to talk your boss into restarting the company? You'd be better off working on solving the *problem* of finding a new job or starting your own business. People with a positive attitude often lose a job and use it as an opportunity to transition to something better. People who spend time and energy trying to solve a predicament just get frustrated.

More than twenty-five years ago when I was dealing with some difficult issues, I wrote something to help me see problems in the right light. It became my new "definition" of problems. Maybe it will help you too:

P redictors—helping to mold our future.

R eminders—showing us that we cannot succeed alone.

O pportunities—pulling us out of ruts and prompting us to think creatively.

B lessings—opening doors we would otherwise not go through.

L essons—providing instruction with each new challenge.

E verywhere—telling us that no one is excluded from difficulties.

M essages—warning us about potential disaster.

S olvable—reminding us that every problem has a solution.

If you can separate the predicaments from the problems, then you put yourself in a much better position to deal with the predicaments and to solve the problems.

2. Anticipate Problems

A young man sent a cryptic e-mail home to his mother at the end of his second college semester. It said, "Flunked out of school and coming home tomorrow. Prepare Dad." It wasn't long before he received an equally brief reply: "Dad prepared. Prepare yourself!"

Al Davis, owner of the NFL's Oakland Raiders, says, "A great leader doesn't treat problems as special. He treats them as normal." If you're working, expect problems. If you're dealing with family, expect problems. If you're just minding your own business and trying to relax, expect problems. If everything goes according to plan, then be pleasantly surprised. If it doesn't and you've planned accordingly, then you won't get so frustrated. A problem not anticipated is a problem. A problem anticipated is an opportunity.

3. FACE THE PROBLEM

About twenty years ago, a television commercial ran that showed a family at home. The children were playing, the mother was vacuuming, and the father was reading the paper. They could be seen as a typical American family except for one problem: There was a huge elephant in the room with them. Even though you could see that it was making things difficult for them, and they were having to move around it, they seemed to be ignoring the elephant, pretending it didn't exist. The ad was for alcoholism awareness. Difficult problems such as alcoholism create chaos in families, yet people often pretend that everything's fine and won't address the problem.

Author and former economic planner John Perkins believes, "There are three kinds of people in our society: those who can't see or refuse to see the problems; those who see the problems and because they didn't personally create them are content to blame someone else; and those who see the problems and though they didn't create them are willing to assume personal responsibility for solving them."

In my decades of experience working with people, I've found that when people face adversity, they make one of these four decisions:

Flee it—they try to get away, but problems always follow.

Forget it—they hope the problem will go away, but problems left alone only get worse.

Fight it—they resist, but the problems still persist.

Face it—they look at the problem realistically.

People who face their problems understand that the first step in solving a problem is to begin.

4. EVALUATE THE PROBLEM

It's said that if you keep your head when all about you are losing theirs—then you don't understand the problem. Seriously though, if a serious problem doesn't cause you to pause and take stock, then you probably haven't evaluated it properly. And that will create difficulties for you down the road, because if you've misjudged the size or scope of a problem and try to deal with it anyway, you will have to stop in the middle of trying to solve it, reevaluate, and start all over again.

Mike Leavitt, United States secretary of health and human services under President George W. Bush, says, "There is a time in the life of every problem when it is big enough to see, yet small enough to solve." The trick is to find the right timing and then to be patient when implementing the solution. Inexperienced people expect problems to be settled instantly. Experienced people are like the master sculptor who keeps striking at the chisel on the marble block with steady blows of the hammer. Unlike the rookie who expects to split the stone with one blow of the hammer, he knows that if he keeps working at it, he will eventually succeed.

5. Embrace Each Problem as a Potential Opportunity

President John F. Kennedy was once asked how he became a war hero. His response: "It was quite easy. Somebody sunk my boat!" While it is true that certain individuals have a vision for innovation or change and they pursue it with purpose, the majority of the time adversity paves the way for success. That was the case for King Gillette, who was so tired of sharpening his straight razor that he developed the safety razor with disposable blades. It was true for Chester Greenwood, who suffered from frostbitten ears and consequently developed earmuffs. It was true for Humphrey O'Sullivan, a printer, who tired of coworkers who kept stealing the rubber mat he stood on to work and finally created rubber heels for his shoes. And it was the case for a man whose small shop was in tough straits financially. He recalled,

> I was paying a sheriff $5 a day to postpone a judgment on my small factory. Then came the gas man, and because I could not pay his bill promptly, he cut off my gas. I was in the midst of certain very important experiments, and to have the gas people plunge me into darkness made me

so mad that I at once began to read up on gas technique and economics, and resolved I would try to see if electricity couldn't be made to replace gas and give those gas people a run for their money.[2]

That man was Thomas Edison, founder of the Edison General Electric Company, which later became General Electric.

Problems are wake-up calls for creativity. If we choose to wake up and get up, problems will prompt us to use our abilities, rally our resources, and move us forward. When a person has the difference maker, adversity causes him to draw on and develop greater strength.

Problems are wake-up calls for creativity.

6. THINK OF PEOPLE WHO HAVE BIGGER PROBLEMS

In a *Peanuts* cartoon, Snoopy sees that everyone in the family is inside the house enjoying Thanksgiving dinner while he receives dog food. *How about that?* he thinks to himself. *Everyone is eating turkey today, but just because I'm a dog, I get dog food.*

He walks to his doghouse, climbs on top, and thinks,

suddenly gaining perspective. *Of course*, Snoopy realizes, *it could have been worse. I could have been born a turkey.*

How big or difficult our problems appear to be is often a matter of perspective. Most difficulties we face are pretty insignificant in the big scheme of things. When a friend gets cancer or loses a loved one, *then* we are reminded of how petty our issues are.

Writer James Agee recalled how he once struck up a conversation with an impoverished elderly woman in the heart of Appalachia during the Great Depression. She lived in a tiny shack with dirt floors, no heat, and no indoor plumbing.

"What would you do," he asked, "if someone came along and gave you some money to help you out?"

The old woman thought for a moment and answered, "I guess I'd give it to the poor."[3]

7. LIST ALL THE POTENTIAL WAYS TO SOLVE THE PROBLEM

Richard Wirthlin worked as President Ronald Reagan's pollster when he was in the White House. During those years, the president's approval rating varied widely. Right after the assassination attempt on Reagan's life, his rating was about 90 percent. A year later, in the midst of the recession of 1982, his numbers plummeted. Wirthlin recalls having to deliver those low figures to Reagan.

"Well, how was it? How are they? What do the figures look like?" the president asked.

"Well, they're pretty bad, Mr. President."

"How bad are they?"

"Well," answered Wirthlin, "they're about 32 percent."

"Dick, don't worry," said the president with a smile. "I'll just go out there and try to get shot again."[4]

Author and speaker Grenville Kleiser stated, "To every problem there is already a solution whether you know what it is or not." I would take that another step further. I believe every problem has *many* solutions, and no problem can stand the assault of sustained thinking.

To solve problems, we need to fire up our creativity, apply sustained thinking, and pull together our resources. Included in those resources are people. The problems that surround us are not as crucial as the people around us. As you think about solutions, consider the people of your acquaintance who might be able to help you.

8. Determine the Best Three Ways to Solve the Problem

An older woman was being tried for the murder of her

third husband. A lawyer asked, "What happened to your first husband?"

"He died of mushroom poisoning," said the woman.

"How about your second husband?"

"He died of mushroom poisoning too," she replied.

"Well then," the lawyer continued, "what about your third husband?"

"He died of a brain concussion."

"How did that happen?" asked the lawyer.

"He wouldn't eat the mushrooms."

Good thinkers always have more than one way to solve a problem. I believe people make mistakes when they think there is only one solution to any problem. If you identify the *three* best solutions to any problem, you give yourself options—and a backup plan in case the first solution fails.

9. Refocus on the Mission

Ralph Waldo Emerson observed, "Concentration is the secret of strength in politics, in war, in trade, in short, in all management of human affairs." Where should you focus that concentration? On the mission. And when you make a mistake, don't chase after it. Don't try to defend it. Don't throw good money after it. Just refocus your attention on the mission and then move on. You must always keep your eye on what it is you desire to do. I have yet to meet a person focused on yesterday who had a better tomorrow.

John Foster Dulles, secretary of state in the Eisenhower administration, observed, "The measure of success is not whether you have a tough problem to deal with, but whether it is the same problem you had last year." A problem solved is a springboard to future success, to bigger and better things. The key is to focus on what you are learning, not on what you are losing. If you do that, then you will open the door to future possibilities.

> *"Positive thinking is how you think about a problem. Enthusiasm is how you feel about a problem. The two together determine what you do about a problem."*—NORMAN VINCENT PEALE

The difference maker can help you do that. It can help you learn from the present and look to the future. Norman Vincent Peale said, "Positive thinking is how you think about a problem. Enthusiasm is how you feel about a problem. The two together determine what you do about a problem." And that's what really matters in the end.

HOW YOUR ATTITUDE CAN BE THE DIFFERENCE MAKER CONCERNING PROBLEMS

Take one or two minutes to make a list of the top ten things you've done in your life about which you are most proud. Do not take into account what others might say are your greatest accomplishments. This is *your* list. And do not try to rank them. Simply write the first ten you can think of very quickly.

1. _____

2. _____

3. _____

4. _____

5. _____

6. _____

7. _____

8. _____

9. _____

10. _____

Now that you've completed your list, I'm willing to bet that your successes came after you experienced . . .

1. A problem (or challenge)
2. Self-doubt
3. Commitment to persevere

In retrospect, we generally remember the problem and the commitment, but we forget that we also experienced a season of self-doubt. We forget that we had to change our thinking before we could change the problem. And that takes the difference maker—your attitude. When facing problems, remember to always start with yourself.

EIGHT

Fear

On March 4, 1933, Franklin Delano Roosevelt was sworn into office as the thirty-second president of the United States. It was a dark time in American history because the country was in the worst part of the Depression. Unemployment was at 25 percent, many families' savings accounts had been wiped out by bank failures, and farmers were losing their land to foreclosure. People were having trouble feeding their families. To help reassure the people of the country, during his first inaugural address, Roosevelt uttered words that have now become famous:

Let me assert my firm belief that the only thing we have to fear is fear itself—nameless, unreasoning, unjustified terror which paralyzes needed efforts to convert retreat into advance. In every dark hour of our national life a leadership of frankness and vigor has met with that understanding and support of the people themselves which is essential to victory. I am convinced that you will again give that support to leadership in these critical days.[1]

What most people did not know is that the president had personally experienced some dark hours in which fear paralyzed him. Roosevelt was born a child of privilege and was educated in Europe, at Harvard, and at Columbia Law School. In his late twenties, be became a state senator and followed his term in office serving as assistant secretary of the navy. But in 1921 at age thirty-nine, Roosevelt was stricken with a severe case of polio that left him severely debilitated.

During his recovery, Roosevelt developed an extreme fear of fire. He worried that he would not be able to escape a fire because of his disability. But in time, Roosevelt overcame his fear. He regained the use of his hands, and he even learned to walk again with the aid of braces. And he reentered the political arena—fearlessly campaigning to become the governor of New York, which he did in 1929. He went on to become one of the nation's greatest presidents.

FEAR IS PART OF THE HUMAN CONDITION

We tend to think that successful people somehow are exempt from experiencing fear, but nothing could be further from the truth. Every generation in human history has experienced fear. It goes all the way back to Adam and Eve. After they disobeyed God and He called to them, Adam answered, "I heard Your voice in the garden, and I was afraid because I was naked; and I hid myself."[2]

Fear is part of human nature, and it always has been. Trace through human history and you can find plenty of quotes on fear. Here are just a few:

- Lucretius (ca. 60 B.C.) "For as children tremble and fear everything in the blind darkness, so we in the light sometimes fear what is no more to be feared than the things children in the dark hold in terror and imagine will come true."

○ Michel Eyquem de Montaigne (1580) "The thing I fear most is fear."

○ Francis Bacon (1623) "Nothing is terrible except fear itself."

○ Duke of Wellington (1831) "The only thing I am afraid of is fear."

People today are also fearful. According to psychiatrist James Reich, 3 percent of all Americans experience panic, 6 percent agoraphobia, 3 percent generalized anxiety, 2.5 percent simple phobias (fear of a specific situation, object, creature, experience, or activity), and 1.5 percent social phobias (dread of situations that involve interaction with other people).[3] That means one in six people have serious issues with fear. On a lighter note, a psychiatrist who was guest on the original *Tonight Show* told host Steve Allen, "The only two really instinctive fears in men are the fear of loud noises and the fear of falling." He then asked, "What are you afraid of, Mr. Allen?" The host's response: "I have a great fear of making a loud noise while falling."

Of course, most people's fears are more ordinary. Surveys done by the Barna Research Group indicate that four out of five adults face major difficulties in life

which really concern them. Their worries break down
this way:

Finances 28%
Health 19%
Career concerns 16%
Parenting struggles 11%
Family relationships 7%
Accomplishing personal goals 7%[4]

Your greatest fears may not be included in this list,
but I'm certain that you experience some kind of fear.

THE DESTRUCTIVE EFFECTS OF FEAR

Fear can be a very destructive force in a person's life.
The root of the word *fear* comes from the Old English
word *fær*, literally meaning a sudden attack, and is akin
to the Old High German word *fāra* meaning ambush or
snare.[5] That's what fear does to us: It attacks us and
makes us captive. As psychiatrist and Nazi concentration camp survivor Viktor Frankl observed, "Fear makes
come true that which one is afraid of."

The destructive power of fear, if left unchecked, can be devastating. Here are just some of the negative things fear can do in a person's life:

1. FEAR BREEDS MORE FEAR

The most insidious thing about fear is its ability to exaggerate itself. C. Everett Koop, former surgeon general of the Unites States, observed, "People have an inappropriate sense of what is dangerous." If you're not convinced about that statement, then think about this. Are you afraid of flying? Did you know that you are more likely to die choking on a piece of food than in a commercial airline crash? Afraid of dying in a robbery? You are twice as likely to be killed playing a sport than you are to be stabbed to death by a stranger. Are you afraid of sharks? Every year barnyard pigs kill more people than sharks do. Worried about having surgery? You are sixteen times more likely to die in a car crash than you are to die of complications from surgery.

Seldom does the thing we fear come to pass. In our minds, we project coming disasters that will likely never occur. And when they don't come to pass, we think, "Phew, that was a *close* one!" when the reality is that our own thoughts were the only thing creating potential danger for us.

2. FEAR CAUSES INACTION

A census taker was going far into a rural area to finish the work in his territory. Driving down the country roads, he saw many houses with "Beware of Dog" signs. At the gate of the last address on his list, he saw another "Beware of Dog" sign as he entered a farmyard near a barn.

Afraid to get out of his car, he honked his horn, and soon a man came out of the barn with a small Chihuahua at his heels.

When the census taker was done asking his questions and filling out his paperwork, he mentioned how many beware-of-dog signs he had seen and asked, "Is this the dog all the signs are about?"

"Yup, sure is," the farmer replied, picking up the friendly dog.

"But that dog couldn't keep anyone away."

"I know," said the farmer, "but the signs sure do." The lesson is that fear is like a warning sign that makes us afraid of a dog that cannot hurt us!

People who let some kind of fear get hold of them

find themselves increasingly more fearful. It can create a debilitating cycle. Here's how this often works.

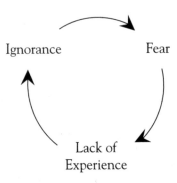

Fear makes us afraid of doing something that might be beneficial for us. Taking action will require us to move into the unknown. That can be scary. But if we give in to our fear, we don't move forward. We don't receive the benefit of what we avoided, nor do we gain the valuable experience that would make us better informed. As a result, we remain ignorant about that area of life, and ignorance almost always breeds more fear, making it that much harder to push ahead and get things done.

We cannot allow fear to paralyze us. As John F. Kennedy observed, "There are risks and costs to a program of action, but they are far less than the long-range risks and costs of comfortable inaction." If we are too afraid of failure, we probably will never win. If we are afraid to die, we will hardly live. Everything in life has some degree of risk.

3. Fear Weakens Us

Harry Truman, thirty-third president of the United States, remarked, "The worst danger we face is the danger of being paralyzed by doubts and fears. This danger is brought on by those who abandon faith and sneer at hope. It is brought on by those who spread cynicism and distrust and try to blind us to our great chance to do good for all mankind."

Fear and anxiety are debilitating emotions. They are interest paid in advance on a debt you may never owe. And they undermine faith—in ourselves, in others, and in God.

Fear	Faith
Weakens	Strengthens
Imprisons	Liberates
Paralyzes	Empowers
Disheartens	Encourages
Sickens	Heals

Nineteenth-century preacher and author C. H. Spurgeon stated, "Our anxiety does not empty tomorrow of its sorrows, but only empties today of its strengths." A person cannot allow fear to master him and become the master of his strengths at the same time. It just doesn't happen.

4. FEAR WASTES ENERGY

An old German adage says, "Fear makes the wolf bigger than he is." Because of that, when people let fear get hold of them, they expend valuable energy in ways they shouldn't. How? Sometimes they avoid things that can't really harm them, like the man who returned to his vacation cabin from a hike badly scratched and bruised.

"What happened?" asked his wife.

"I met a snake on the trail," the man answered.

"Don't you remember?" the woman responded. "The ranger told us yesterday that none of the snakes up here are poisonous."

"They don't have to be poisonous if they can make you jump off a twenty-foot cliff!"

Clearly the man's fear—not the snake—was the problem.

Other times people waste energy fantasizing about solutions to problems they fear *will* come their way.

Ironically, what started as an unfounded fear can turn into a real problem because a person wasted energy on wishful thinking instead of productive action. Joe Tye, author of *Never Fear, Never Quit*, says,

> Wishful thinking is the lock that fear puts on the prison gate. Fear lets you indulge yourself, for a while, in flights of wishful thinking. Somehow, you think, something will happen to make the problems go away. By the time you wake up, it's too late. What you feared has happened, and fear has defeated you. The only way to escape from the prison of fear is action. You cannot wish your way out, you cannot wait your way out. You can only work your way out. Every time you escape the prison of fear, you grow stronger.[6]

The bottom line is that fear can push you in the wrong direction by producing nervous energy that causes you to do your worst in a new situation, or it can sap your energy as you fight its paralyzing effects.

5. FEAR KEEPS US AND OTHERS FROM REACHING OUR POTENTIAL

Psychologist Randall B. Hamrock observed, "In twenty years [of practice as a psychologist], I've talked with, tested, and given vocational counsel to at least 10,000 young men and women. One characteristic that almost all had was the tendency to sell themselves short." Fear robs us of our potential. It makes us smaller than we really are. One of the greatest mistakes we can make in life is to be in constant fear that we will make one.

When we give in to fear, we are already beaten. People who are ruled by fear stay where it's safe. And that's sad because people can't reach their potential by staying where it's safe. Worse yet, they keep others from reaching their potential too. When a leader is ruled by fear, he becomes a lid to the people who follow him. Many people fail to reach their potential because their leaders are fearful.

A story from U.S. history illustrates this well. During the American Revolution, the Bahamas were captured by Spain. In April of 1783, Andrew Deveaux, a lieutenant colonel of South Carolina, recruited a handful of militiamen and Harbour Island settlers and planned to take Nassau using a clever strategy.

Deveaux had only two hundred men with him, a far smaller force than that of the Spanish, but he managed to capture the high ground on the island after a brief skirmish. The Spaniards then watched as boats repeatedly ferried load after load of men from Deveaux's ships to his defensive position on shore. What the Spaniards didn't know was that the same men kept going back and forth, standing on their trip over to the island and hiding themselves by lying down in the boat on the trip back to the ships. The leader of the Spanish troops, fearing a defeat at the hands of a large force in a defensible position, surrendered.

Playwright William Shakespeare wrote, "Our doubts are traitors, and they make us lose what we oft might win, by fearing to attempt." That was certainly true in this incident from history.

HOW TO HANDLE FEAR

So how can a person handle fear instead of getting handled by it? If you have been averse to risk and a prisoner of fear, you may be wondering if an individual must possess great courage or exceptional talent. The answer is that fear can be overcome by anyone. Here are the steps I recommend to anyone who is having difficulty moving forward because of fear.

1. ADMIT YOUR FEARS

Several old-timers sat around talking about their days in the old West, when one said, "I'll never forget the time I killed an Indian."

"Shoot him?" asked another old-timer.

"Nope," said the first.

"Kill him hand to hand with a knife?" asked the second man.

"No, nothing like that," answered the first. "Ran him to death."

"How far did you chase him?"

"Didn't," said the first old-timer. "I was in front."

You can't overcome your fears unless you first recognize they exist. Make a list of what makes you feel fear. If you feel unable to do that, you may be running from those feelings. If that is the case, start paying attention to your feelings. When does your heart race for no apparent reason? When are you paralyzed into inaction? When do you display nervous energy for no apparent reason? These kinds of responses may be due to fear.

2. DISCOVER THE SOURCE OF YOUR FEARS

A man who had a morbid fear of thunder went to see a noted psychiatrist for treatment.

"You have a condition called brontophobia," the doctor said to the man. "It's silly to be afraid of thunder at your age. Just think of it as a drumroll in the symphony of life."

"What if that doesn't work?" the man asked.

"Well, then do as I do. When you hear thunder, stuff cotton in your ears, crawl under the bed, and sing 'Mary Had a Little Lamb' at the top of your voice until it stops."

Most people's fears are based not on facts, but on feelings. I think of *fear* as **F**alse **E**xpectations **A**ppearing **R**eal. You have to look beyond the irrational feelings you may possess and discover the expectations that lie beneath them. American humorist James Thurber wrote, "All men should strive to learn before they die what they are running from and to and why." That is the next step in the process.

3. Realize How Your Fears Can Limit You

Philosopher and Catholic cardinal J. H. Newman advised, "Fear not that your life will come to an end but that it will never have a beginning." That's what can happen if you let fear take over your life. Honestly, most of our fears are totally unfounded. In fact, studies have shown that 95 percent of what we fear is baseless. The rest are simply things we must learn to live with. Maybe the best approach is to adopt the attitude of poet Gertrude Stein, who said, "Considering how dangerous everything is, nothing is really frightening."

> *Studies show that 95 percent*
> *of what we fear is baseless.*

There are no guarantees in life. People look for many things to protect them: burglar alarms, traveler's checks, aspirin, umbrellas, GPS systems, and air bags. But the truth is that life is dangerous, damaging to your health, and will eventually kill you. So you might as well live life to the fullest.

4. ACCEPT NORMAL FEAR AS THE PRICE OF PROGRESS
One of the secrets of success is not letting what you cannot do interfere with what you can do. Millionaire entrepreneur and philanthropist W. Clement Stone, who started his business career at age five selling newspapers and was selling insurance full-time at age sixteen, never let fear stop him from being successful. A strong proponent of positive thinking, Stone said that the secret to

making sales was going where you do not want to go and doing what you do not want to do.

I've found this to be true in my own career. Today I am known most for my public speaking. But when I first started speaking, I wasn't effective. I remember being really fearful. Then when I got the chance to speak at an event as a senior in college, I was terrible. People who knew me then described my speaking style as "stiff." But I kept at it. I began to study effective communicators and spoke to small audiences at every opportunity. It took me seven years to become comfortable while speaking. Only then could I develop and hone my communication style.

In time I got chances to speak to larger audiences. The first time I spoke to over a thousand people was at Veterans Memorial Auditorium in Columbus, Ohio, in the 1970s. In the 1980s, I spoke to an audience of more than 10,000 for the first time during a youth rally at the University of Illinois. In the 1990s, I spoke to 68,000 people at the RCA Dome in Indianapolis. And in the 2000s, I've spoken live in events that were simulcast to even larger audiences.

I don't tell you this to brag. I say it because when I was afraid during that first speaking engagement, I had no idea where it would lead me. But I didn't let my fear rule me. Instead, I accepted it as the price I would have to pay for personal progress.

Shakespeare said, "He is not worthy of the honeycomb that shuns the hive because the bees have stings." Don't let your fear keep you from taking small steps in your development. You never know where they might lead.

5. CONVERT FEAR INTO DESIRE

Fight manager Cus D'Amato believed, "The hero and the coward both feel exactly the same fear, only the hero confronts his fear and converts it into fire." Just about every negative emotion we feel can be converted into something positive to help us get further in life.

> Afraid of poverty? Convert it to a positive work ethic.
> Afraid of greediness? Convert it to generosity.
> Afraid of rejection? Convert it to an ability to connect with people.
> Afraid of insignificance? Convert it to the service of others.

Roger Babson, founder of Babson College and Webber International University, remarked, "If things go wrong, don't go with them." Instead, make a new way. People can turn their lives around by taking the very thing that once created fear and using the energy to do something positive and worthwhile.

> *"If things go wrong, don't go with them."*—ROGER BABSON

6. FOCUS ON THINGS YOU CAN CONTROL

Many things in this life you cannot control. There's no good reason to worry about those things. Writer Harold Stephens observes, "There is a great difference between worry and concern. A worried person sees a problem, and a concerned person solves a problem."

How can you become a problem solver? Focus on the things you can control. That usually means two things. The first is your attitude. As you interact with people, you cannot control their actions—no matter how much you might like to. But you can control your attitude. Remember, what happens *to* you isn't as important as what happens *in* you. The second is your calendar. You may not be able to control today's circumstances, but you can do your best to plan the time you have. Most people who fear the future do so because they don't prepare for it.

7. GIVE TODAY YOUR ATTENTION—NOT YESTERDAY OR TOMORROW

Yesterday and tomorrow seem to clamor for our attention. Yesterday wants us to second-guess past decisions and worry if we did the right thing. But that is wasted energy. As President Harry Truman said, "If you've done the best you can—if you have done what you have to do—there is no use worrying about it, because nothing can change it."

The future also can cause us to miss present opportunities. I love what former First Lady Barbara Bush said about the future, comparing it to a train ride:

> We get on board that train at birth, and we want to cross the continent because we have in mind that somewhere out there is a station. We pass by sleepy little towns looking out the window of life's train, grain fields and silos, level grade crossings, buses full of people on the roads beside us. We pass by cities and factories, but we don't look at any of it because we want to get to the station. We believe that out there is a station where a band is playing and banners are hung and flags are wav-

ing, and when we get there that will be life's destination. We don't really get to know anybody on the train. We pace up and down the aisles looking at our watches eager to get to the station because we know that life has a station for us.

This station changes for us during life. To begin with, for most of us, it's turning 18, getting out of high school. Then the station is that first promotion and then the station becomes getting the kids out of college, and then the station becomes retirement and then . . . all too late we recognize the truth—that this side of that city whose builder is God, there really isn't a station. The joy is in the journey and the journey is the joy.

Sooner or later, you realize there is no station and the truth of life is the trip. Read a book, eat more ice cream, go barefoot more often, hug a child, go fishing, laugh more. The station will come soon enough. And as you go, find a way to make this world more beautiful.[7]

Most people arrive at a different destination than they expect in life—some better, some worse, but all different. So focusing on the destination is not a good idea. Besides, tomorrow may come; it may not. There are no guarantees.

The only place we really have any power is in the present. Do what you can in the here and now—despite your fear—and you will have the satisfaction of knowing that you are doing everything within your power to reach your potential.

> *"I've been through some terrible things in my life, a few of which actually happened."*—MARK TWAIN

8. FEED THE RIGHT EMOTION AND STARVE THE WRONG ONE

In life, both faith and fear will arise within you, and you choose which one will prevail. Someone once wrote,

Two natures beat within my breast,
The one is foul, the other blessed.
The one I love, the other I hate;
The one I feed will dominate.

The thing is, both of those emotions will *always* be present in you. The emotion you continually feed is the one that will dominate your life. You can't expect fear simply to disappear. If you continually focus on your fears, entertain them, and give in to them, they will increase. The way to ultimately overcome them is to starve them. Don't give your fears any of your time or energy. Don't feed them with gossip or negative news shows or frightening movies. Focus on your faith and feed it. The more energy and time you give it, the stronger it becomes. And anytime you feel afraid of doing something but go ahead and do it anyway, you will be reprogramming your attitude. When you feel fear, it will mean "go" instead of "stop," and "fight harder" instead of "give up."

I opened this chapter writing about how Franklin D. Roosevelt overcame great obstacles, including fear, to become a world leader. Eleanor Roosevelt, his wife, was also a high achiever and leader in her own right. When her husband was struck down by polio, she not only nursed him back to health, she kept his political aspirations alive by becoming involved in New York state politics on his behalf. She promoted human rights causes while Franklin was president, and after mourning his death became a delegate to the United Nations. She once wrote, "You gain strength, courage and confidence by every experience in which you really stop to look fear in the face. You are able to say to yourself, 'I lived through this horror. I can take the next thing that comes along.' You must do the thing you think you cannot do."

That is what overcoming fear may be to you—doing what you think you can't. But no matter how strong a hold fear may try to take on you, it can be overcome, because fear is in your mind, and your mind can be changed using the difference maker—your attitude.

HOW YOUR ATTITUDE CAN BE THE DIFFERENCE MAKER CONCERNING FEAR

How much of a factor is fear in your life? To what degree does it dominate your attitude? Rate yourself according to the fear index. Circle the number that best corresponds to how you feel about fear:

1. I don't remember the last time I was really afraid even though I take significant risks on a daily basis.
2. I am afraid rarely and only when I or someone close to me is physically in danger; I take reasonable risks and manage my anxiety well.

3. I am a little more fearful than I would like to be, and if I had more courage, I would do more of the things I would really like to do in life.
4. Fear is a significant factor in my everyday life; I avoid anything that I would consider risky or dangerous.
5. I am afraid of many things on a daily basis, and it changes the way I live my life.

Here's what I recommend you do according to how you rated yourself:

If you circled number 1, you are an unusual individual who does not experience normal fear, maybe even when in dangerous situations. You may have to temper your actions with greater discernment and wisdom.

If you circled number 2, you have a good attitude toward fear and possess an excellent handle on it. You should try to encourage others who have a more difficult time with fear than you do.

If you circled number 3 or number 4, you are in an excellent position to improve your life by changing your attitude toward fear. Begin by identifying the source of your fears and determining to turn your fear into fire. For each area of fear, figure out its positive opposite and then create a plan of action to cultivate that quality. Then focus on what you can control *today*. And don't forget that fear is the normal price for progress.

If you circled number 5, then fear is really getting the better of you, and you will have a difficult time over-coming it on your own. Talk to a counselor, clergyman, or doctor to get advice on how to proceed.

NINE

Failure

When it comes to failure, I have to agree with Jan Christian Smuts, a prime minister of South Africa in the first half of the twentieth century who desired to dismantle the country's apartheid system. He said, "A man is not defeated by his opponents but by himself." Most people don't need to learn more about how to overcome their rivals. They need to learn how to get out of their own way.

SELF-SABOTAGING BEHAVIORS

There are three types of people in this world: the "wills," the "won'ts," and the "can'ts." The first type accomplish everything. The second oppose everything. The third fail at everything. People who accomplish much certainly are competent, but their attitude also makes a huge difference. A positive attitude will definitely help you avoid being part of the second group. And if you learn how to handle failure correctly, you'll be able to keep yourself out of the third group.

What tends to pull people into the "can't" group? Most of the time, there are four things:

1. EXPECTING FAILURE

The Law of Human Behavior says, "Sooner or later we will get what we expect." Usually, the people who keep failing are the ones who expect to. They're like the pessimist whose tombstone epitaph read, "I expected this."

> *Sooner or later we will get what we expect.*
> —THE LAW OF HUMAN BEHAVIOR

In her autobiography, actress Helen Hayes wrote about the Thanksgiving when she cooked her first turkey. Before serving it, she made an announcement to her husband and son.

"Now I know this is the first turkey I've ever cooked," she said. "If it isn't any good, I don't want anybody to say a word. We'll just get up from the table, without comment, and go out to a restaurant to eat."

Hayes then went back to the kitchen and returned to the dining room with the turkey. There she found her husband and son seated at the table—with their hats and coats on.[1]

2. Personalizing Failure

People cannot perform in a way inconsistent with the way they see themselves. Everybody fails. But people who continually fail expect to fail and usually *see themselves as failures*. There's a big difference between failing and being a failure.

Sportswriter Grantland Rice observed, "Failure isn't so bad if it doesn't attack the heart. Success is all right if it doesn't go to the head." If you want to maintain a good attitude and be successful, you cannot take your failures—or your successes—too personally. That's always a danger. But as you get older, more experienced, and more confident, you realize that your failures aren't fatal, and your successes don't completely define you.

3. REFUSING TO TAKE A RISK

Life means risk. People who sabotage themselves shouldn't worry about failure as much as they should be concerned about the chances they miss when they don't even try. Speech writer Charles Parnell observed, "Too many people are having what might be called 'near-life experiences.' They go through life bunting, so afraid of failure that they never try to win the big prizes, never knowing the thrill of hitting a home run or even taking a swing at one."

French writer, poet, and art critic Guillaume Apollinaire wrote,

> Come to the edge.
> No, we will fall.
> Come to the edge.
> No, we will fall.
> They came to the edge.
> He pushed them and they flew.

Those who fly always first get out on the edge. If you want to seize an opportunity, you must take a risk. If you want to grow, you must make mistakes. If you want to reach your potential, you will have to take chances. If you don't, you will be resigned to a life of mediocrity. The people who don't make mistakes end up working for those who do. And in the end, they often end up regretting the safe life they lived.

4. LETTING FAILURE DEFEAT THEM

After a particularly bad defeat, legendary baseball manager Casey Stengel remarked, "You gotta lose 'em sometimes. When you do, lose 'em right." Everybody experiences losses. But not everybody allows himself to be stopped by those losses. We must prepare ourselves for failure. We should train for it, preparing to bounce back from it when it occurs. As professional snooker player Steve Davis says, "It may not be your fault for being down, but it is your fault for not getting up." That's what people with the right attitude do—they get back up and keep trying.

> "*It may not be your fault for being down, but it is your fault for not getting up.*"—*Steve Davis*

HOW TO PROFIT FROM FAILURE

If you can't avoid failure, yet you're also not supposed to give in to it and let it color your thinking, what do you do with it? The answer is profit from it. Several years ago I wrote a book called *Failing Forward*. The thesis of the book was that the difference between average people and achieving people is their perception of and response to failure. What creates the right perception and response? The answer is the difference maker. When you have the right attitude, you can actually use failure to your advantage and profit from it. Here's how:

1. CHANGE YOUR ATTITUDE

Cartoon character Homer Simpson summarized the attitude of millions of people when he said, "Kids, you tried your best and you failed miserably. The lesson is, never try." Homer is the classic underachiever. In another episode, he stated, "Trying is the first step toward failure." Homer never tries, and like many real people, he'll be stuck where he is forever.

Business staffing pioneer Robert Half observed, "Laziness is a secret ingredient that goes into failure. But it's only kept a secret from the person who fails."

People who succeed develop an attitude of tenacity. They refuse to quit, and they are determined not to let failure defeat them. If you desire to fulfill your dreams, achieve your goals, and live life to the fullest, that's the kind of attitude you need to cultivate.

2. Change Your Vocabulary

A noted psychiatrist once remarked that the two saddest words in the human vocabulary are "if only." He believed that people who get trapped in their failures spend their whole lives saying "if only—if only I had tried harder, if only I had been more kind to my kids, if only I had been more truthful, if only . . ." The way to correct that mind-set is to change your vocabulary by substituting the words "next time"—"next time I will try harder, next time I will be more kind to my kids, next time I will be more truthful."

Failure isn't failure if you do better the next time. In *Leaders on Leadership*, Warren Bennis interviewed seventy of the nation's top performers in numerous fields. None of them used the word *failure* to describe their mistakes. Instead they referred to learning experiences, tuition paid, detours, or opportunities for growth.[2] You may think that's a small difference, but that small difference can make a big difference. The way you think determines how you act.

Failure isn't failure if you do better the next time.

3. PAY LITTLE ATTENTION TO THE ODDS

You may feel that the odds are stacked against you in life. So what! Every person who has ever achieved something significant had to overcome the odds. The problem for most people isn't the odds. It's that they sell themselves too short. R. H. Headlee observed, "Most people think too small, aim too low, and quit too soon."

When it comes to the thing you love to do, the thing you were made to do, aim high. The odds matter little. Whether you fall down along the way matters little. You fell when learning to walk, didn't you? Maxwell Maltz, developer of psycho-cybernetics, says, "You are a champion in the art of living if you reach only 65 percent of your goals." If the odds say you will make a lot of mistakes on the way to success, so be it. As long as you are eventually successful, isn't that what matters? Remember, if at first you don't succeed, then know that you're running about average.

4. LET FAILURE POINT YOU TO SUCCESS

Oliver Goldsmith was born the son of a poor preacher in Ireland in the 1700s. Growing up, he wasn't a great student. In fact, his schoolmaster labeled him a "stupid blockhead." He did manage to earn a college degree, but he finished at the bottom of his class. He was unsure of what he wanted to do. At first he tried to become a preacher, but it didn't suit him, and he was never ordained. Next he tried law but failed at it. He then settled on medicine, but he was an indifferent doctor and was not passionate about his profession. He was able to hold several posts only temporarily. Goldsmith lived in poverty, was often ill, and once even had to pawn his clothes to buy food.

It looked like he would never find his way. But then he discovered an interest and aptitude for writing and translating. At first, he worked as a Fleet Street reviewer and writer. But then he began to write works that came out of his own interests. He secured his reputation as a novelist with *The Vicar of Wakefield*, a poet with "The Deserted Village," and a playwright with *She Stoops to Conquer*.

My friend, Tim Masters, says that failure is the productive part of success. It provides the road you don't have to travel again, the mountain you don't have to climb again, and the valley you don't have to cross again. At the time you're making mistakes, they may not feel like "the kiss of Jesus," which was Mother Teresa's term for failures that drive us to God. But if we have the right attitude, they can lead us to what we ought to be doing.

5. HOLD ON TO YOUR SENSE OF HUMOR

One of the best things you can do for yourself when you fail is to learn to laugh. I love the comment made by a humorist who said he spoke for an organization where they always rated the previous meeting's speaker in their program using little bells. Speakers who received a standing ovation got four bells next to their name. Those who were above average got three. Merely average speakers got two bells, and poor speakers got one. The humorist said that when he spoke to them several months ago, they awarded him the no-bell prize.

There isn't a person alive who wouldn't benefit from a good laugh, especially when he's done something really stupid. When you take your mistakes too seriously, then everything seems to become life-and-death. When that happens, you sure die a lot. The way to solve that is to keep your sense of humor no matter how bad things get.

6. LEARN FROM YOUR MISTAKES

Successful restauranteur and celebrity chef Wolfgang Puck said, "I learned more from the one restaurant that didn't work than from all the ones that were successes." Isn't that usually the way it is? I know that I've learned more from my failures than from my successes—the times that I've had the right attitude about them. When I didn't try to make excuses or place the blame on others, I always learned. That's why I love this quote from Robert Kiyosaki, author of *Rich Dad, Poor Dad*. He says, "Sometimes you win and sometimes you learn."[3] That's the mark of a great attitude! You don't lose—you learn.

> "*Sometimes you win and sometimes you learn.*"—ROBERT KIYOSAKI

7. DON'T LOSE YOUR PERSPECTIVE

When ethicist and theologian Reinhold Niebuhr prayed the now famous "Serenity Prayer," he was preaching in a little church in Massachusetts. Only a small group of people was in the audience that day, but one person liked the prayer and after the service asked him for a copy.

"Here," Niebuhr responded, handing over a crumpled piece of paper. "I doubt I'll have any more use for it."

That simple prayer went on to become the most published prayer in America, and Alcoholics Anonymous adopted it.[4] It's ironic that Niebuhr's prayer became so popular. Evidently his perspective wasn't good because he didn't know what he had.

When Football Hall of Fame coach Don Shula was head coach of the Miami Dolphins, he used to practice a twenty-four-hour rule. He allowed himself, his players, and his coaches only twenty-four hours after a game to celebrate a victory or lament a loss. Once the twenty-four hours had passed, it was time to think about getting ready for the next game. That kind of perspective made Shula one of the most successful coaches in NFL history.

Failure is just like success—it's a day-to-day process, not someplace you arrive one day. Failure is not a one-time event. It's how you deal with life along the way. True, you will make mistakes, but you can't conclude that you're a failure until you breathe your last breath. Until then, you're still in the process, and there is still time to turn things around.

8. DON'T BECOME TOO FAMILIAR WITH FAILURE

In a *Peanuts* comic strip, Lucy misses yet another fly ball. As she approaches Charlie Brown on the mound to explain, she says, "I thought I had it, but suddenly I remembered all the others I've missed." Then Lucy sums up with the ultimate in excuses: "The past got in my eyes." Clearly, Lucy has become way too familiar with failure.

I once heard somebody say that winning is coming in fourth exhausted but excited because you came in fifth last time. That's the right way to think about failure. If you let your mistakes get you down and you stop trying, then you've taken up residence in the house of failure. That's a place nobody ought to live.

9. MAKE FAILURE A GAUGE FOR GROWTH

If you were a baseball fan during the early 1960s, you probably remember a Los Angeles Dodger named Maury Wills. From 1960 to 1966, Wills was a record-making base stealer. In the 1962 season alone, he stole 104 bases!

Wills set another record during that time: most times being thrown out while stealing. In 1965, a year in which he stole more bases than any other player in the major leagues, he also held the record for times caught stealing: thirty-one times.

Most baseball enthusiasts don't remember Wills' failures; they remember only his successes. But if Wills had allowed himself to become discouraged by his outs, he would not have continued to attempt steals, and he never would have set any records.

Successful people understand the role failure plays in achievement. That's true in any life endeavor. Inventor Thomas Edison said, "I'm not discouraged because every wrong attempt discarded is another step forward." And gold-medal-winning gymnast Mary Lou Retton asserted, "Achieving that goal is a good feeling, but to get there you have to also get through the failures. You've got to be able to pick yourself up and continue." Whether it's thousands of experiments that don't work or thousands of falls from a balance beam, the milestones on the road of success are always failures. The farther you go, the more failures you experience.

> *"The person interested in success has to learn to view failure as a healthy, inevitable part of the process of getting to the top."*—JOYCE BROTHERS

Psychologist Joyce Brothers observed, "The person interested in success has to learn to view failure as a healthy, inevitable part of the process of getting to the top." You have to learn to actually see failure as a friend, a companion to success. If you're not failing, then you probably aren't really moving forward. You're just doing what's familiar, comfortable, and safe. As actor Mickey Rooney said, "You always pass failure on the way to success."

10. NEVER GIVE UP

A young man who had just gone off to college decided to bring a female friend he was thinking of dating home to meet his mom. When his friend did not meet his mom's approval, he quickly cooled to the idea of dating her and brought another girl home, hoping for better luck. But this girl didn't meet Mom's standards either. One by one, he brought every girl he knew home, and not a one of them met his mom's approval.

Fed up, he went looking for a girl exactly like his mother. She was the same height, had the same coloring, and even had similar mannerisms. *Surely*, he thought, *she won't have any objections to* this *girl*. And he was right. Mom loved her. There was only one problem: Dad didn't!

Failure doesn't mean you'll never succeed. It just

means it will take longer. John Wayne utters a great line in the movie *The Train Robbers*. He says, "You're going to spend the rest of your life getting up one more time than you're knocked down, so you'd better start getting used to it." That's what success is—getting up one time more than you fall. You have no idea how close you may be to what you desire to achieve. If you give up, you will never know—and you guarantee that you will never get there. Author, lawyer, economist, and actor Ben Stein says, "The human spirit is never finished when it is defeated. It is finished when it surrenders." My advice is: don't ever give up!

> *Failure doesn't mean you'll never succeed.*
> *It just means it will take longer.*

About twenty years ago, *Time* magazine described a study by a psychologist of people who had lost their jobs three times due to plant closings. The writers were amazed by what they discovered. They expected the people being laid off to be beaten down and discouraged. Instead they found them to be incredibly resilient. Why was that? They concluded that people who had weathered repeated adversity had learned to bounce back. People who had lost a job and found a new one twice before were much better prepared to deal with adversity than someone who had always worked at the same place and had never faced adversity.[5]

It may sound ironic, but if you have experienced a lot of failure, you are actually in a better position to achieve success than people who haven't. When you fail, and fail, and fail again—and keep getting back up on your feet and keep learning from your failures—you are building strength, tenacity, experience, and wisdom. And people who develop such qualities are capable of sustaining their success, unlike many for whom good things come early and easily. So if you've failed a lot, celebrate. As long as you don't give up, you're in a really good place.

HOW YOUR ATTITUDE CAN BE THE DIFFERENCE MAKER CONCERNING FAILURE

It's hard to put failure in the right perspective if you are continuing to engage in self-sabotaging behaviors. Answer the following four questions honestly:

1. **Expectations:** What's usually the forecast for your day—cloudy or sunny? Are you someone for whom most things generally go right or wrong? What percentage of the time do you expect to succeed at things you do day to day? Mark your answer on the line below.

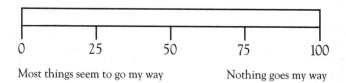

Most things seem to go my way   Nothing goes my way

2. **Self-Image:** How do you see yourself when it comes to failure? This may be a difficult thing to discern. Do you believe you are a highly competent and successful person who sometimes fails, or are you basically a failure who is working to avoid mistakes?

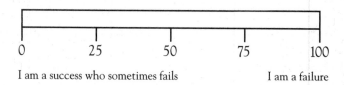

I am a success who sometimes fails   I am a failure

3. **Risk:** What is the role of risk in your life? Is risk a normal and healthy part of achieving success, or is it something to be avoided at all cost? Perhaps the best

way to discern the way you really feel is to ask the question this way: What percentage of the time do you seek comfort, safety, peace, and the status quo?

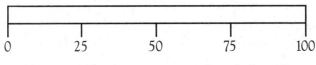

| 0 | 25 | 50 | 75 | 100 |

I seek out reasonable risks   I avoid risks at all costs

4. **Tenacity:** Think about the top four or five priorities in your life. If you can't name them off the top of your head, then give the subject some thought and jot them down. In what percentage of those priorities have you lost intensity and stopped fighting to improve and succeed? If you're not sure, use the following as a gauge: If you have not seen a significant improvement in the last year, then you are probably not adequately pushing yourself to succeed in that area.

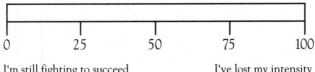

| 0 | 25 | 50 | 75 | 100 |

I'm still fighting to succeed   I've lost my intensity

If you marked a number higher than 25 percent for any of the questions, then you may be exhibiting self-sabotaging behavior. Use the following list of questions to help change your thinking the next time you experience failure.

○ Did I fail because of another person, because of my situation, or because of myself?
○ Did I actually fail, or did I simply fall short of unrealistic expectations?
○ What part of this "failure" was successful?
○ What lessons can I learn from this?
○ Am I grateful for the experience despite the outcome?
○ Is there a way to turn the failure into a success—for myself or others?
○ Have people I know had a similar experience; if so, can they help me?
○ How can I use my experience to help others avoid similar problems?
○ Where do I go from here?

TEN

The Difference Maker in Your Life Can Help You Make a Difference in the Lives of Others

Attitude isn't everything, but it is one thing that can make a difference in your life. I genuinely believe that, and hopefully by now you have discovered that those words are not only true but also potentially life-changing. People who are successful don't have fewer challenges than anyone else. At this point you probably realize that successful people experience more failure, overcome more problems, navigate more changes, and deal with more potential discouragement and fear than those who don't succeed. How do they do that? They let the difference maker make the difference!

Recently I received a letter from Kevin Keup, president of K. Keup Concrete Construction in Batavia, Illinois, describing how he made some major changes in his life. Here's what he wrote:

Dear Sir,

Two years ago on Father's Day I received your book *The Power of Attitude* as a gift from my wife. As I looked through it, one passage stopped me. On page 23, the quote is, "A pessimist is a person who, regardless of the present, is disappointed in the future." That hit me like a ton of bricks. It referred to the person I had unknowingly become. I didn't know I was at that negative place until I read those words, and I was forced to reckon with who I had become.

I had been in business for 29 years at that point, and for 28 of those years I was an optimist. Whatever difficulties came my way, when I went to bed I knew tomorrow would be a better day. At some point I changed. That phrase in your book was a real trigger for me. Acknowledging that I was living in deep pessimism became a turning point for me and started a journey of change in my life.

I have been renewed spiritually, emotionally, and physically during this journey over the last 2 years. As a business owner, I have a unique opportunity to communicate my thoughts with the people who work with me. One thing that we have implemented here is including a passage from your book and other sources with each week's payroll for about 40 people.

We work in the construction industry, and having these messages go out to our men has been powerful and has brought about positive change. Some of the men keep the quotes on their refrigerators or on bulletin boards to share with their families. . .

All this started with your book and the power of that particular phrase, and I just want to thank you.

Sincerely,
Kevin Keup

When a person recognizes that his attitude isn't right, it opens the door for positive change and tremendous opportunity.

HELPING YOU—HELPING OTHERS

I want to leave you with a few important thoughts as you finish this book and prepare to harness the power of the difference maker in your life and that of others.

1. MAKE THE DECISION TO ALLOW THE DIFFERENCE MAKER TO MAKE A DIFFERENCE IN YOUR LIFE

Never forget that your attitude is a choice. You are the only person who can decide to harness the power of the difference maker. As you ponder that decision, consider this:

> There is a choice you have to make in everything you do.
>
> So keep in mind that in the end, the choice you make makes you.

For many people in this world, the difference maker will never make a difference. Why? They have chosen an attitude that is not an asset to them. If someone isn't purposely choosing to have the right attitude, then she is choosing to have the wrong attitude.

2. MANAGE YOUR DECISION EVERY DAY OF YOUR LIFE

The choices we make in life don't *stay* chosen by themselves. In my book *Today Matters*, I point out, "Successful people make right decisions early and manage those decisions daily." Decision making is important. We can't change and grow without it. But decision managing is highly underrated. We think that our good decisions will automatically stay good, but they won't. Every right decision we make must be managed every day. Remember what Kevin Keup said in his letter? He said he had "unknowingly become" a negative person—even after twenty-eight and a half years of being a positive person!

His was a management issue. He had failed to manage his attitude. And I've learned through experience that it's easier to *maintain* a right attitude than it is to *regain* it! Every day, begin your day by consciously choosing to manage your attitude as a positive influence in your life.

> *It's easier to maintain a right attitude*
> *than it is to regain it.*

3. DO NOT ALLOW ADVERSITY TO HAVE AN ADVERSE EFFECT ON YOUR ATTITUDE

Everybody can have a good attitude when things are going well. But what happens to you when situations in your life go bad? Think back to the Big Five Attitude Obstacles in the book: discouragement, change, problems, fear, and failure. Which one is most likely to affect you negatively? Are you continually preparing yourself to meet its challenges? You have to be ready mentally to keep difficulties from defeating you.

In September of 2005, Hurricane Katrina left a devastating mark on the southern United States. A few days after the storm hit, an article appeared in *USA Today* containing advice to the people of the American Gulf Coast from people who had suffered similar tragedies. Here's what it said:

> Veterans of some of the nation's worst natural disasters in recent years offer these words of advice for Hurricane Katrina's victims:
>
> Be patient. "It will probably take longer to recover than you think," says Curt Ivy, city manager in Homestead, Fla., ground zero for Hurricane Andrew in 1992. "We thought we would be back in three to five years. We really didn't have a clue."
>
> Beware of shady contractors. "You know there's going to be every Tom, Dick and Harry fly-by-night contractor in New Orleans," says Bob Boucher, whose Houston home was flooded by Tropical Storm Allison in 2001. Don't pay in advance for materials, and don't pay in full before the work is done.
>
> Save your money. If you're out of work, consider call-

ing creditors and putting them on hold rather than paying your bills on time. "What you need is cash until these things pass," says Stan Thomas, who lost his mortgage business in the 1994 Northridge earthquake that hit Southern California.

Prepare for a shortage of labor and materials. Anticipate your needs, such as concrete, Sheetrock, shingles—and people to do the work.

Lean on others, including counselors and churches. "The biggest thing is being able to rely on a close network of friends, family, really pulling together," says Jacob Spenn, who manages the Tropical Storm Allison Recovery Project in Harris County, Texas. "The tighter communities are the communities that seem to come out of it faster."

Go slow and have faith. "Don't do anything real quick," says Phil Halstead, who lost his house to a tornado in Oklahoma City six years ago. "Initially, you think, 'There's just no way I'm going to get out of this,' but you will. You got to stay tough mentally, because it could sure wear you down."[1]

Notice that much of the advice given by people who survived other tragedies focused on attitude issues: Be patient, be wary, prepare yourself, lean on others, have faith, and stay mentally tough. These veterans of adversity are essentially saying, "You couldn't control Katrina, and you can't control your circumstances, but you *can* control your attitude. If you do, it will make a difference in your life. It can be the difference maker between giving up and bouncing back."

4. ONCE THE DIFFERENCE MAKER MAKES A DIFFERENCE IN YOUR LIFE, HELP OTHERS DISCOVER THE DIFFERENCE MAKER IN THEIR LIVES

I want you to notice one more thing about the letter from Kevin Keup. He's not keeping his discovery about the power of a positive attitude to himself. He's sharing the difference maker with his employees because he knows it will help them. And the result is that the difference maker is starting to spread through the company and make a difference there.

Anyone who helps others discover the impact of the difference maker helps himself, helps others, and makes his little corner of the world a better place to live. Who wouldn't want to be around people who believe in themselves and others, have hope, and work positively to solve problems and overcome difficulties?

I've been writing books for almost thirty years now, and I will keep doing so for one reason: I want to add value to people. Sometimes people like Kevin write me to say that a book I've written has made a difference in their lives. Most of the time, the people whose lives are positively impacted never tell me. That's okay.

Recently my friend Carole Bos shared with me the story of someone who made a difference in her life and how she desperately wants to let him know about the impact he had made. I was so intrigued that I asked her to write it out for me so that I could share it with you. Here is her story:

It was one of those damp winter nights when the wind, blowing off the North Sea, made me long for a fireplace and a good book. Instead, I had to write a final exam.

We lived in a flat with no fireplace. I was twenty-one years old, trying simultaneously to learn Dutch and German. My professor, on sabbatical from USC, was wrapping up his year of teaching German in the Netherlands. The night of the exam would be the last time I'd see him before he returned to the States.

At the end of class, the prof dismissed everyone but asked me to stay for a few minutes: "I'd like to grade your exam before you leave." I thought it an odd request but obliged him. I had no idea he was about to change my life.

As he handed my graded exam back to me, that USC prof said, "Carole, I want to talk with you about your future. I've taught at USC a long time. I've had lots of students pass through my classes. You are one of the brightest of those many students, but you do not know that about yourself. As you leave here tonight, I want you to remember my words: You can do anything you want to do. You can be anything you want to be. But you first need to believe in yourself. You need to change your attitude about what you can personally accomplish. Before we part ways, I want you to promise me you will do that."

His words were burned in my memory when I realized he had no motive other than my best interests. I told Jim, my husband, about our conversation.

"He's right," Jim observed. "I think you should study law and become a lawyer." I ultimately took the advice of both.

Working hard in college, juggling both a job and school, I managed to graduate at the top of my class. During law school, I clerked at a firm where I learned to be a courtroom lawyer. After graduation, looking forward to a career with Juris Doctor degree in hand, I was crushed. The firm hired all the male clerks as permanent lawyers. As for me, the only clerk who'd made *Law Review*: "Women shouldn't be trial lawyers." In order to be a courtroom lawyer, I had to start my own firm.

Twenty-five years later, I am blessed with a great team at Bos & Glazier where we work with wonderful clients. I have had the privilege of handling many interesting cases throughout the country, writing inspirational books and giving motivational talks. My great sadness is that I've been unable to carry our children to term. But using my love of storytelling, my degrees in history and Russian studies, and my trial-lawyer skill in finding primary sources, I am able to touch the lives of children everywhere through AwesomeStories.com. It is used in schools throughout the States (as an online teaching/learning tool) and in seventy-five countries (as a fun way for people to improve their English).

I would like to let my USC professor know he became one of the top five most influential people in my life. The problem is . . . I no longer remember his name.

Countless millions of people are like that professor. Every day they add value to others, and there is a very high probability that in most cases they will never be told that they made a difference. That's also okay. This army of difference makers understands that success each day should be judged by the seeds they sow, not the harvest they reap.

> *Success each day should be judged by the seeds sown, not the harvest reaped.*

Won't you join us in this crusade to make a difference in the lives of others? I believe you will. As the author, I hope this book will make a difference in your life. As you lay it down, I am hoping you will make a difference in the lives of others. That is what *The Difference Maker* is all about. Godspeed!

Notes

Chapter 1: Where Did You Get Your Attitude?

1. Bob Conklin, *The Dynamics of Successful Attitudes* (New York: Prentice-Hall, 1963).
2. Howard Baker, "Frankl, Victor E. (1905-1997)," obituary, *Gale Encyclopedia,* http://www.findarticles.com/p/articles/mi_g2699/is_0004/ai_2699000472 (accessed September 15, 2005).
3. Pamela Jessica Runyon, "Viktor E. Frankl," *Empire:zine,* http://www.empirezine.com/spotlight/frankl/frankl1.htm (accessed September 15, 2005).

Chapter 2: What Your Attitude *Cannot* Do for You

1. Sharon Jayson, "Yep, Life'll Burst That Self-Esteem Bubble," *USA Today,* February 15, 2005, http://www.usatoday.com/life/lifestyle/2005-02-15-self-esteem_x.htm (accessed September 14, 2005).
2. Ibid.
3. Bill Hybels, *Courageous Leadership* (Grand Rapids, MI: Zondervan, 2002), 84.
4. "Positive Attitude Delays Aging," BBC News World Edition, September 12, 2004, http://news.bbc.co.uk/2/hi/health/3642356.stm (accessed September 15, 2005).
5. http://www.getmotivation.com/favorites12.html.

6. "Peter Jennings," Wikipedia, http://en.wikipedia.org/wiki/ Peter_Jennings (accessed September 19, 2005).
7. Ibid.

Chapter 3: What Your Attitude Can Do for You
1. Denis Waitley, *The Winner's Edge* (New York: Berkley, 1986).
2. Ernest H. Rosenbaum and Isadora R. Rosenbaum, "Attitude— The Will to Live," Cancer Supportive Care Programs National and International, reprinted from *Coping with Cancer*, March/April 1999, http://www.cancersupportivecare.com/ attitude.html#Mind (accessed September 23, 2005).
3. Ibid.
4. John Milton, *Paradise Lost, Book I*, line 253.

Chapter 4: How to Make Your Attitude Your Greatest Asset
1. quoted at http://www.eyeforbeauty.com/Personal/Philosophy/ life.html.
2. Norman Vincent Peale, *The Power of the Plus Factor* (New York: Ballantine, 1996).
3. Adidas ad, *ESPN: The Magazine*, February 16, 2004.

Chapter 5: Discouragement
1. Adapted from "How You Can Tell When It's Going to Be a Rotten Day," http://www.joke-archives.com/toplists/rottendy.html .
2. Charles Bracelen Flood, *Lee: The Last Years* (New York: First Mariner Books, 1998) 136.
3. *The Megiddo Message*.
4. "Colonel Harland Sanders," about KFC, www.kfc.com/about/ colonel.htm.
5. Napoleon Hill, *Think and Grow Rich* (New York: Ballantine, 1987).
6. Eliza Strickland, "Happy Birthday 'Leaves of Grass,'" http://jscms.jrn.columbia.edu/cns/2005-02-15/strickland- waltwhitman (accessed November 1, 2005).
7. D. Martyn Lloyd-Jones, *Spiritual Depression: Its Causes and Cure* (Grand Rapids, MI: Wm. B. Eerdmans Publishing Company, 1965), 20.
8. Lucy Maher, "Are You Too Hard on Yourself?"

9. Exercise Regimen for the Workplace," http://www.
   ucolick.org/~de/humour/exercise.html

Chapter 6: Change
1. David Bayles and Ted Orland, *Art and Fear* (Santa Barbara:
   Capra Press, 1993), 57.
2. Frances Hodgson Burnett, *The Secret Garden* (New York: Harper
   Trophy, 1998), 337.

Chapter 7: Problems
1. Tom Zuercher, "And Let it Begin with Me,"
   http://www.brethren.org/AC2001/Zuercher.htm.
2. *Forbes*, October 16, 1920, https://www.keepmedia.com/
   Auth.do?extId=10022&uri=/archive/forbes/2005/1017/044.html.
3. "Bits and Pieces," August 9, 2001, 21.
4. Richard Reeves, *President Reagan: The Triumph of Imagination*
   (New York: Simon and Schuster, 2005).

Chapter 8: Fear
1. Franklin D. Roosevelt, Inaugural Address, March 4, 1933, as
   published in Samuel Rosenman, ed., *The Public Papers of Franklin
   D. Roosevelt, Volume Two: The Year of Crisis, 1933* (New York:
   Random House, 1938), 11–16, quoted on http://historymatters.
   gmu.edu/d/5057/ (accessed November 26, 2005).
2. Genesis 3:10, NKJV.
3. James Reich in *Journal of Nervous and Mental Disease*, March
   1986, quoted in Robert Handly and Pauline Neff, *Beyond Fear*
   (New York: Rawson Associates, 1987), 9.
4. Barna Research Group, "Most Americans Satisfied with Life
   Despite Having Quality of Life Issues," March 26, 2002,
   http://www.barna.org/FlexPage.aspx?Page=BarnaUpdate&Barna
   UpdateID=109 (accessed November 26, 2005).
5. *Webster's New World Dictionary of American English, 3rd College
   Edition* (Cleveland, OH: Simon and Schuster, 1991).
6. Joe Tye, author of *Never Fear, Never Quit* (New York: Delacorte
   Press, 1997).
7. Barbara Bush, Address to Kennebunk (Maine) High School,
   source unknown.

Chapter 9: Failure
1. Helen Hayes, *On Reflection: An Autobiography* (New York: M. Evans and Company, 1968).
2. Warren Bennis, *Leaders on Leadership* (Boston: Harvard Business School Press, 1992).
3. Robert Kiyosaki, *Rich Dad, Poor Dad* (New York: Warner Business Books, 2000).
4. Harold C. Warlick Jr., *Conquering Loneliness* (Waco, Tex: Word Books, 1979).
5. Arthur Freeman and Rose DeWolf, *The 10 Dumbest Mistakes Smart People Make and How to Avoid Them: Simple and Sure Techniques for Gaining Greater Control of Your Life* (New York: HarperCollins, 1992).

Chapter 10: The Difference Maker in Your Life Can Help You Make a Difference in the Lives of Others
1. Richard Wolf, "Words of Advice from Fellow Survivors," *USA Today*, September 12, 2005, A6.

About the Author

John C. Maxwell is an internationally recognized leadership expert, speaker, and author who has sold over 12 million books. His organizations have trained more than one million leaders worldwide. Dr. Maxwell is the founder of Injoy Stewardship Services and EQUIP. Every year he speaks to Fortune 500 companies, international government leaders, and organizations as diverse as the United States Military Academy at West Point and the National Football League. A *New York Times*, *Wall Street Journal*, and *Business Week* best-selling author, Maxwell was one of 25 authors named to Amazon.com's

10th Anniversary Hall of Fame. Two of his books, *The 21 Irrefutable Laws of Leadership* and *Developing the Leader Within You*, have each sold over a million copies.

June 08